SEX. MAYHEM. WHATEVER.

THE INDEPENDENT MOVIE POSTER BOOK

Spencer Drate   Judith Salavetz

Text by Dave Kehr

Foreword by Sam Sarowitz

From the Collection of the Posteritati Gallery

Harry N. Abrams, Inc., Publishers

Project Manager: Céline Moulard

Editor: Virginia Beck

Jacket design: Elliott Earls

Designers: Judith Salavetz and Spencer Drate, Arlene Lee

Poster transparencies by Jellybean Photographics and Imaging

Production Manager: Norman Watkins

Library of Congress Cataloging-in-Publication Data
Drate, Spencer.
The independent movie poster book / Spencer Drate and Judith Salavetz ; text by
David Kehr ; from the collection of Posteritati.
p. cm.
Includes bibliographical references and index.
ISBN 0-8109-9190-X (pbk. : alk. paper)
1. Film posters–Catalogs. I. Salavetz, Judith. II. Kehr, David. III. Posteritati (Firm)
IV. Title.
PN1995.9.P5D73 2005
016.79143'75–dc22
                          2004020413

Published in 2004 by Harry N. Abrams, Incorporated, New York
All rights reserved. No part of the contents of this book may be
reproduced without the written permission of the publisher.

Printed and bound in China

10 9 8 7 6 5 4 3 2 1

Harry N. Abrams, Inc.
100 Fifth Avenue
New York, N.Y. 10011
www.abramsbooks.com

Abrams is a subsidiary of LA MARTINIÈRE

Spencer and Judith would like to thank:

All of the independent movie companies and directors who contributed
to our book and whose creative and independent films inspired these
wonderful posters. Thanks also go to Dave Kehr; Sam Sarowitz at the
Posteritati Gallery; Michael Jacobs, Harriet Whelchel, Céline Moulard,
Michael Walsh, Peter Lowry, Ron Longe, Jessica Napp, Nicholas
Gaudiuso, and everyone at Abrams; Jeff Dowd, "The Dude"; Dean Rink
and Tamie Lynn; Ned and Alexis Davis; Justin and Ariel Kavoussi;
Michael Bonfiglio, Matt Mahurin and Metallica; Nancy Hennings, Evan
Shapiro, and everyone at IFC; and Jellybean Photograpics and Imaging
for the perfect movie-poster visuals.

We have always had an affinity for art books showcasing new genres of innovative design. Independent films have stimulated a wave of fresh design ideas that complement and accentuate the diversity and creativity shown by filmmakers. Although it's probably true generally that the poster does not the movie make, many independent poster artists have demonstrated remarkable ability to capture the essence of their subject films in their designs, and thereby helped draw an ever-expanding audience. We recognized early on that the best posters are not necessarily for films by the most famous directors, so we have strived to balance our selections to reflect both great poster art about obscure films, and great films with interesting poster art. We hope this book will serve as a useful reference for independent film enthusiasts.

Judith Salavetz
Spencer Drate

New York City, September 2004

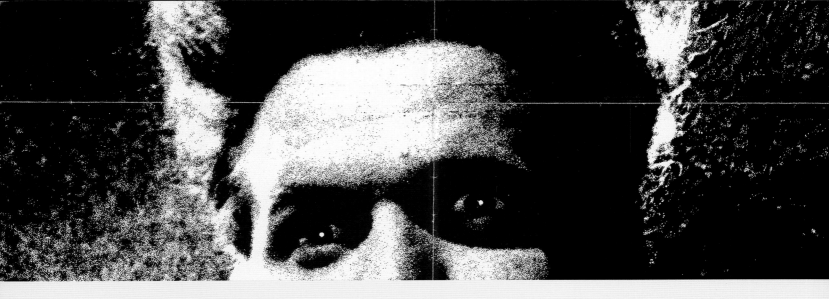

CONTENTS

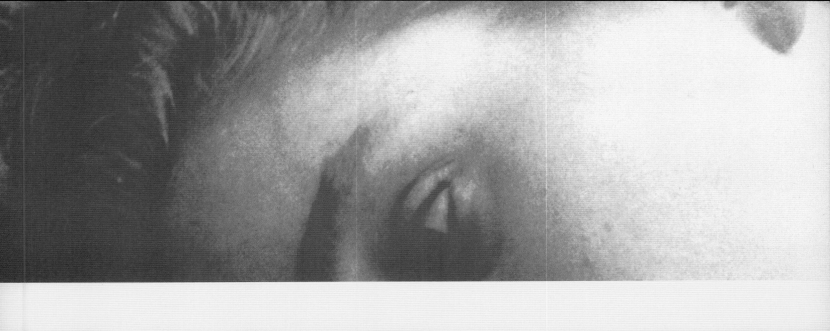

FOREWORD

Good independent movie posters, like good indie movies, evoke the feeling of being outside the mainstream. The originality of the image captures and holds you, leaving you with a visceral impression. The best of them stand alone as art whether you have seen the movie or not.

I started collecting posters by accident. In the mid-1970s I worked after school for legendary film journalist Mo Wax at *Film Bulletin* magazine in Philadelphia. Mo would occasionally dip into his jumbled stockpile of ephemera and give me the odd poster or the latest James Bond stills, which I thought were amazing. The next thing you know, I was hooked.

Many of the posters I treasured in those days seem tame to me now. In the 1960s and 1970s, unimaginative photographic images began replacing the classic artwork formerly featured in Hollywood posters. Posters for independent "art" films, most of foreign origin, were traditionally plain and usually saddled with long reviews. Prior to the 1980s' indie film explosion, American-made independent films were usually released by small distributors with minimal budgets. This often resulted in simple, straightforward posters printed in a hurry (as an example, the poster for *Who's That Knocking at My Door?*, which can be seen in this book). Happily, there were exceptions. For example, posters for *Eraserhead* and *Pink Flamingos* (both included herein) expressed visual flair.

Hollywood movie posters of that era still occasionally displayed a brilliance of their own. A few great illustrators managed to work within the Hollywood system and turn out striking designs. During the 1950s, director Otto Preminger worked with famed artist Saul Bass, who created amazing posters for *Saint Joan* and *Anatomy of a Murder*, among others. Bob Peak (*My Fair Lady, Apocalypse Now*), Robert McCall (*2001: A Space Odyssey*), and Richard Amsel (*The Sting*) are some of

those who also produced outstanding work in the 1960s through the 1980s. At the other end of the scale, low-budget horror and sci-fi movies were responsible for many of the most interesting poster designs of the 1950s to the 1960s. Legend has it that the small companies producing these films would spend more on the poster than on the production itself. This might help to explain *Attack of the 50-Foot Woman*, an almost unwatchable film with a dynamic poster by Reynold Brown.

Unfortunately, the last thirty years have seen a proliferation of boring photographic pastiche posters coming out of Hollywood that look like they were slapped together in some marketing department meeting with thirty people giving their opinions. Of course, many of the films coming out of Hollywood feel the same way!

Independent films, on the other hand, have inspired some outstanding poster art over the last several decades. Since the popular success of *Sex, Lies, and Videotape* in 1989, indie films have repeatedly proven their commercial viability, leading independent production companies to invest more time and money in ad campaigns. At the same time, the experimental nature of many independent films has offered adventurous poster designers an opportunity to explore the limits of their form.

Companies such as Miramax, New Line, Fine Line, First Run Features, Zeitgeist, and the late lamented Cinecom, October Films, and Cowboy Pictures, among others, produced many wonderful posters, several of which are presented in this book. While I love all the examples we have selected, some personal favorites include the advance poster for *Dancer in the Dark*, with its starkly dramatic "eye chart" style graphics; *Pulp Fiction*, which mimics the cover of a well-worn dime-store paperback with distressed edges; *Poison*, with its striking use of color, design, and photography; and *George Washington*

which captures something of the film's poetry with its simple, yet memorable, design.

Independent movies have inspired some of the most creative work by poster designers in Europe and Asia as well, many of which are also represented in this book. While several countries have adopted the practice of copying American poster art for the local release of Hollywood blockbusters, independent films remain more likely to receive a distinctive treatment that reflects a singular tradition and style. Many feature more imaginative designs than the U.S. posters produced for the same film.

British artists have long displayed a strong cutting edge in their designs. Perhaps this stems from the tradition of the famed Ealing Studios, which was renowned in the fifties for its classic poster artwork. The poster in this book for *I Stand Alone* was created by the famed British sensation artist brothers Dinos and Jake Chapman. The best French, Italian, and German posters, on the other hand, exhibit the traditionally beautiful and dramatic art that you might expect from European design. Among the dynamic examples in this book that come from these countries is the French poster for *The State of Things* by designer Guy Peellaert.

Eastern European posters are known for their bold avant-garde designs, a style I find particularly appealing. Polish and Czech posters (for example, *My Own Private Idaho* and *Stranger Than Paradise*) have developed an international reputation and have received numerous design awards. In fact, Poland has evolved into a center for the international recognition of poster art. In 1968, the first poster museum opened outside of Warsaw, and today the Warsaw Biennial remains the oldest and most influential poster exhibition in the world. The Polish poster continues to play a key role in establishing poster design as an art form all its own.

The Hong Kong posters for the Wong Kar Wai films (*Chungking Express*) are wonderfully imaginative, as are the Spanish posters for Pedro Almodóvar's films (*Law of Desire, High Heels, Talk to Her, All About My Mother*, and *Pepi, Luci, Bom*). Both directors most likely have a hand in the designs of the posters from their native lands.

Many Japanese poster designers (most of whom go unnamed) are unique in their use of photo-montage, often producing startling results (*Shadows, 8 1⁄2 Women*). The Japanese posters in this book for the David Cronenberg films *Naked Lunch* and *Spider* represent exceptions to that rule by using surreal artwork, as does the *Madadayo* poster, which was drawn in crayon by the film's renowned director, Akira Kurosawa.

In all, this book features over 200 posters from sixteen countries. Selecting them was not easy. Some well-known independent films that lacked strong graphics in their posters did not make their way into the book. But we have tried to provide you, the reader, with a good cross-section of the best international independent movie posters from 1980 to August of 2004 (our photo deadline), focusing on those that feature especially interesting or unusual designs.

To the extent we've succeeded, I'd like to thank my collaborators, Spencer Drate and Judith Salavetz, who walked in the front door of Posteritati one day with the concept for this book, and Dave Kehr, a very talented writer and an accomplished film historian. I also need to acknowledge the hard work by the wonderful staff at Posteritati, Michael Brydon, Jamie Jarrard, and Stanley Oh for all their help. Lastly to Lauren Gill for her endless good ideas and my son, Benny, who makes every day a joy.

And thank you Mo Wax, wherever you are.

Sam Sarowitz, Posteritati, New York City

DAYS OF BEING WILD:
THE INCEPTION OF INDEPENDENT FILM

The independent film movement was born on that day in December 1908, when Thomas Edison organized the Motion Picture Patents Company, a trust that licensed Edison's technology to a handful of companies. Those filmmakers who didn't sign up with Edison—and they included the future founders of Universal, Fox, and Paramount—became outlaws. Many of them ran off to the wilds of Southern California to escape having their unlicensed equipment confiscated by Edison's goons. When the trust was dissolved in 1915, the independents became the establishment, and the Hollywood studio system was born—thus touching off another wave of independent revolt.

It's a pattern that has continued until the present day. When a once-feisty independent company like Miramax becomes part of the studio establishment (Miramax is now owned by Disney, and puts much of its effort into making mainstream, Oscar-worthy films), newer companies—like Zeitgeist, Strand, Lion's Gate, and many others—pop up to take over the fringe.

This book celebrates the indepedent film movement that began in the 1980s, when the major studios turned away from the quirky, personal films that had been popular in the late '60s and early '70s (including the early work of Robert Altman, Dennis Hopper, and Bob Rafelson) and toward the mass-market potential represented by blockbusters like *Jaws* and *Star Wars*.

But the foundations for that movement had been laid much earlier, by individual, maverick filmmakers in the United States and Europe who ventured outside the traditional lines of financing and distribution to get their distinctive visions on the screen. In the beginning, we might say, there was John Cassavetes.

John Cassavetes

The founding father of what would become the American independent film movement, Cassavetes began as a Broadway actor. He graduated to small Hollywood roles and developed a distaste for what he saw as the phoniness of Hollywood technique. A guest spot on Jean Shepherd's New York radio show earned him $2,000 in listener donations, enough for Cassavetes to begin filming *Shadows*, an unscripted production about a family of African-American jazz musicians. Released in 1959, *Shadows* became a critical sensation. Cassavetes, after unsuccessfully trying the Hollywood route with *Too Late Blues* (1961) and *A Child Is Waiting* (1963), returned to rough-and-ready indie principles with *Faces* in 1968, starring his wife, Gena Rowlands. A nearly unbroken string of important, innovative films followed up to his death in 1989.

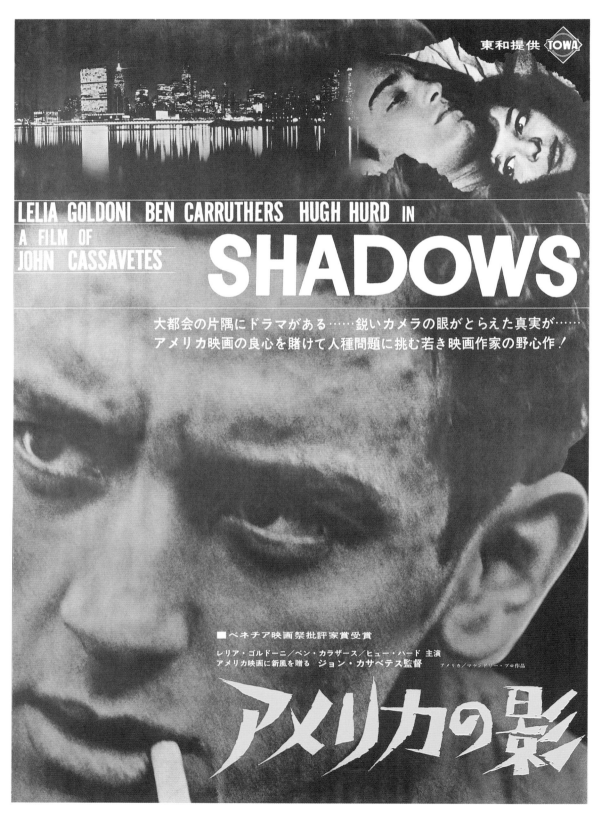

JOHN CASSAVETES
SHADOWS
1959
29 x 20 inches
Japan

Robert Downey

Though he may be best known today as the father of actor Robert Downey, Jr., the elder Downey did much to put independent cinema on the map. His underground satires–like *Chafed Elbows* (1965) and *No More Excuses* (1968)–burst into the mainstream with the commercial success of *Putney Swope* (1969). A satire on the advertising industry, the film introduced taboo subjects like race, sex, and capitalism into American comedy and inspired a generation of irreverent spoofs of contemporary values. Though Downey has continued to direct (most recently, 1997's *Hugo Pool*), his work no longer has the shock value it once did and has suffered accordingly.

"PUTNEY SWOPE"

The Truth and Soul Movie

A Film by Robert Downey. A Cinema V Presentation.

ROBERT DOWNEY
PUTNEY SWOPE
1969
41 x 27 inches
United States

David Lynch

Released in 1978, *Eraserhead* is David Lynch's bizarre, dreamlike hallucination of human sexuality and its unfortunate consequences. The film helped launch the phenomenon known as the "midnight show," where hip crowds gathered after hours in such theaters as New York's Waverly and San Francisco's Castro to celebrate offbeat, transgressive fare. A quarter of a century later, Lynch is still sticking to his guns, though his films—including his masterpiece, *Blue Velvet* (1986)—are now shot in 35mm and surround sound rather than post-dubbed 16mm. A native of Missoula, Montana, and an Eagle Scout as a boy, Lynch has continued to project an All-American image while exploring the intimations of death and kinky sex that lie behind the suburban façade.

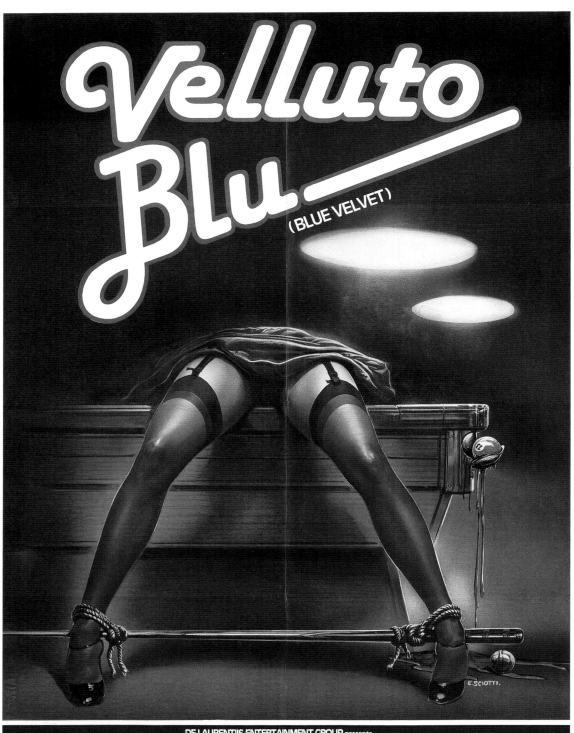

DAVID LYNCH
BLUE VELVET
(*Velluto Blu*)
1986
55 x 39 inches
Italy

DAVID LYNCH   *WILD AT HEART*   1990   30 x 40 inches   Great Britain

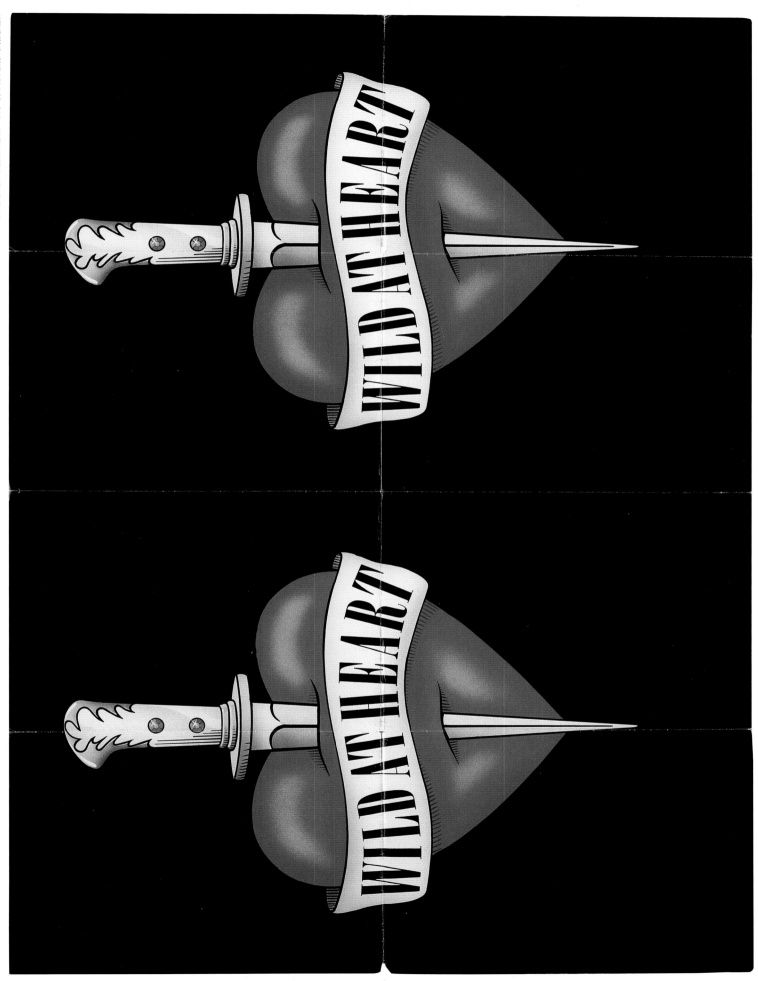

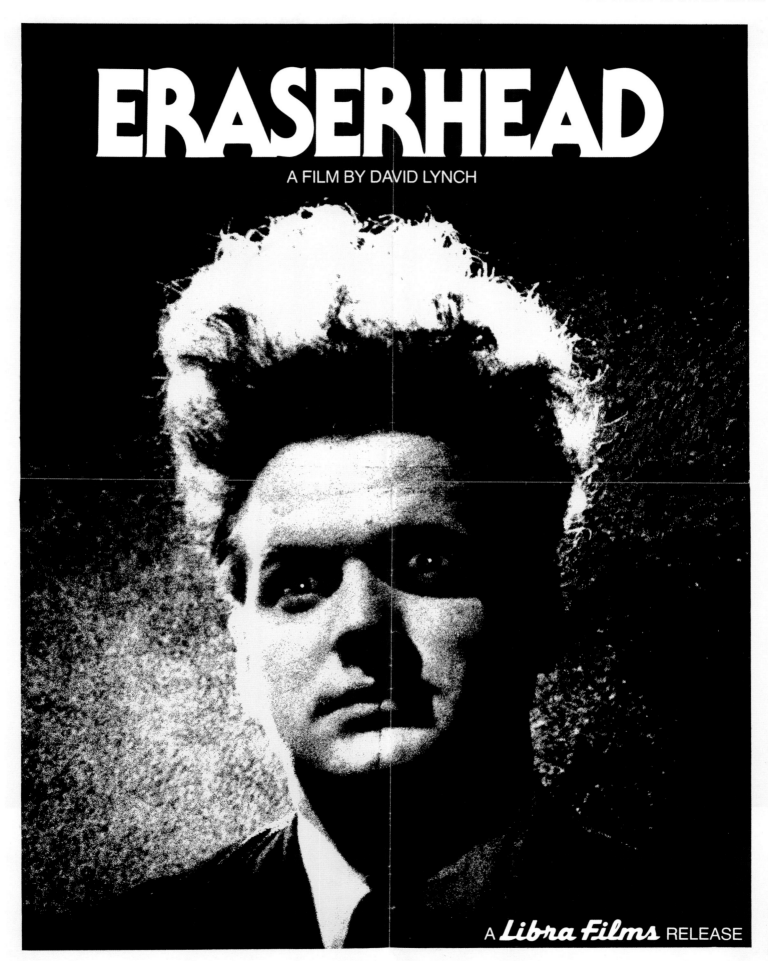

John Sayles

John Sayles's 1980 *Return of the Secaucus 7* was one of the founding gestures of the American independent movement, a warmly realistic study of seven former college radicals reunited as they face new adult responsibilities. The film established the existence of an unsuspected demographic—the young adult—and proved that movies could be made without the technical polish and financial support of major studios. Since then, Sayles's work has rarely been innovative, but he continues to please with his warmly drawn characters (*The Brother from Another Planet* [1984]) and unapologetic "old Left" politics (*Matewan* [1987]).

IT TAKES
MORE THAN
GUNS
TO KILL
A MAN.

JOHN SAYLES
MATEWAN
1987
41 x 27 inches
United States

CINECOM ENTERTAINMENT GROUP AND FILM GALLERY IN ASSOCIATION WITH GOLDCREST PRESENT

MATEWAN A FILM BY JOHN SAYLES STARRING CHRIS COOPER, JAMES EARL JONES, MARY McDONNELL, WILL OLDHAM

DIRECTOR OF PHOTOGRAPHY HASKELL WEXLER PRODUCTION DESIGNER NORA CHAVOOSHIAN EDITED BY SONYA POLONSKY MUSIC BY MASON DARING

EXECUTIVE PRODUCERS AMIR JACOB MALIN, MARK BALSAM, JERRY SILVA ASSOCIATE PRODUCERS IRA DEUTCHMAN, JIM DUDELSON, NED KANDEL

PG-13 PARENTS STRONGLY CAUTIONED PRODUCED BY PEGGY RAJSKI AND MAGGIE RENZI WRITTEN AND DIRECTED BY JOHN SAYLES *Cinecom*
Some Material May Be Inappropriate for Children Under 13

COPYRIGHT © 1987 CINECOM ENTERTAINMENT GROUP INC. ALL RIGHTS RESERVED ORIGINAL SOUNDTRACK ALBUM AVAILABLE ON ROUNDER RECORDS

DESIGNED BY ROSS CULBERT HOLLAND & LAVERY, NYC. PHOTO BY BOB MARSHAK

Martin Scorsese

Only Scorsese's first feature, the 1968 *Who's That Knocking at My Door?*, can be considered an independent production. Still, Scorsese was among the first filmmakers to import the "one man, one film" aesthetic developed by such French filmmakers as François Truffaut and Jean-Luc Godard, a key attitude in independent filmmaking. Moving on to studio productions like *Mean Streets* (1973) and *Raging Bull* (1979), Scorsese remains fascinated by the possibilities of studio production while retaining his faith in a personal, outsider's vision, though of late he seems to have gotten bogged down in expensive period films (*Gangs of New York* [2002], *The Aviator* [2004]) that leave little room for experimentation.

"A NEW CLASSIC ...A GREAT MOMENT IN AMERICAN MOVIES... as a film it has something to say to everyone. A stunning impact, the most evocative descriptions of American life I have ever seen."
—Roger Ebert, Chicago-Sun Times

"SHARP... REWARDING ...attacks the hypocrisy of a religion based double standard."
—Clifford Terry, Chicago Tribune

"Positively Brilliant"
A NEW CLASSIC
who's that KNOCKING at my door

introducing HARVEY KEITEL
starring ZINA BETHUNE as THE NICE GIRL, BUT...
distributed by Joseph Brenner Associates

SELECTED CHICAGO INTERNATIONAL FILM FESTIVAL

MARTIN SCORSESE
WHO'S THAT KNOCKING AT MY DOOR?
1968
41 x 27 inches
United States

John Waters

Never much of a filmmaker, but always a brilliant comic personality, John Waters emerged from Baltimore's bohemian underground with *Pink Flamingos* (1973), the harrowing tale of a competition for the title of "Filthiest Person Alive". The winner–a heavyset transvestite whose stage name was Divine (actually Waters's old high school friend, Harris Milstead)–stooped to conquer by bending over to nibble on a dog's sidewalk surprise. Now his own genre, Waters turns out his bad-taste comedies at the rate of one every two years, briefly breaking into the mainstream with his 1988 musical *Hairspray* (later adapted into a Broadway show).

Wim Wenders

An offspring equally of the French New Wave and American rock music, Wenders began as a chronicler of Europe's alienated youth, with such inspired road movies as *Alice in the Cities* (1974; later, the name he adopted for his production company) and *Kings of the Road* (1977). As Wenders has aged, his work has lost its surly rebelliousness. He has settled into philosophical fantasies, often tinted with supernatural or science-fiction touches, that imagine apocalyptic scenarios–the death of the American dream in *Paris, Texas* (1984); the angelic visitors of *Wings of Desire* (1987); the apocalypse itself in *Until the End of the World* (1991). Wenders's increasing windiness has been balanced by his taste in music, always excellent; his best film in years was the 1999 *Buena Vista Social Club*, which introduced an amazing group of aging, soulful Cuban musicians to the world public.

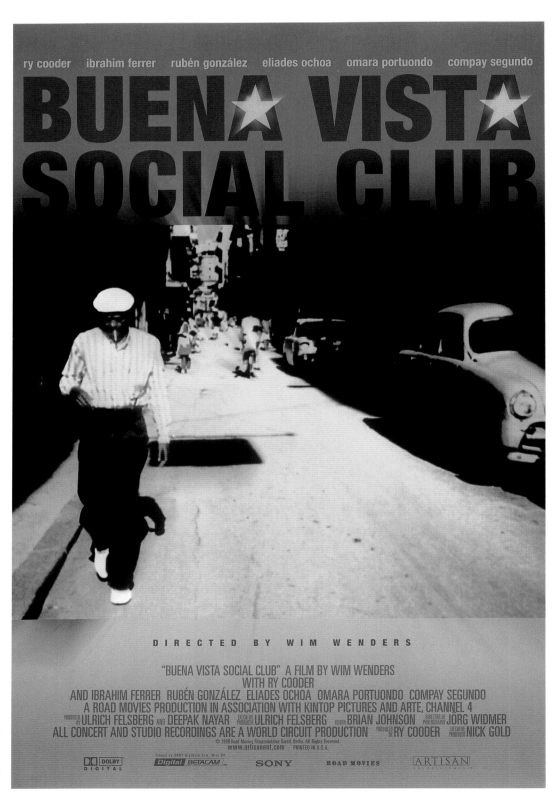

WIM WENDERS
BUENA VISTA SOCIAL CLUB
1999
41 x 27 inches
United States

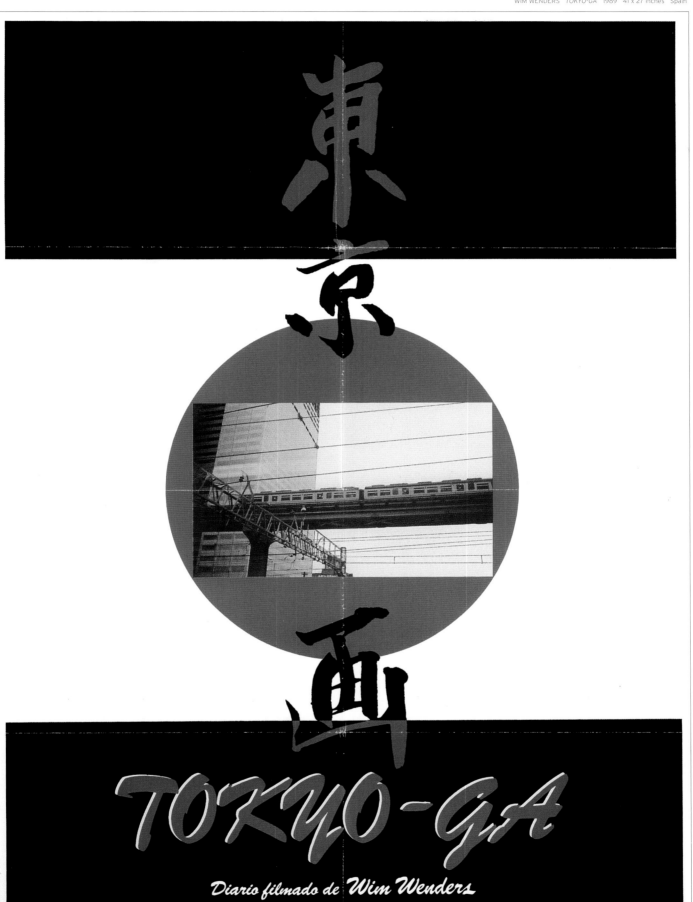

TOKYO-GA

Diario filmado de *Wim Wenders*

con *Chishu Ryu - Yuharu Atsuta - Werner Herzog*

fotografía: *Ed Lachman* - montaje: *Wim Wenders, Solveig Dommartin* - música: *Dick Tracy* - productor: *Chris Sievernich* - guión y realización: *Wim Wenders*
una coproducción de *Wim Wenders Production* y *Chris Sievernich Production* en colaboración con *Westdeutscher Rundfunk*

MUSIDORA

D. L. M - 275 - 1989

I STAND ALONE:
THE INDEPENDENT AUTEUR

The sensibility that shaped the independent film movement of the 1980s was largely inherited from the French New Wave. This group of filmmakers, many of them former critics, emerged in France in the 1960s, proclaiming the primacy of the director in the creative process. Their "one man, one film" rule called for movies as personal as paintings or novels, shaped by individuals and drawn from individual experiences. They were to be the "auteurs"—the authors—of the films that came out under their names.

For many, the birth moment of the current independent scene came when Steven Soderbergh's *Sex, Lies, and Videotape* won the audience award at the 1989 Sundance Film Festival, and followed it up by becoming a major commercial success. But Soderbergh's success was preceded by authors such as the Coen brothers, John Sayles, Wayne Wang, Joyce Chopra, Victor Nunez, Bobby Roth, Jill Godmilow, Jim Jarmusch, and Alan Rudolph.

In the years before and since, many strong, individual voices have risen up to join this group in what has become the blissfully discordant chorus of indie moviemaking. These filmmakers—who generally both write and direct their movies—are usually bigger box-office attractions than the actors in their employ. They have created not work for hire but bodies of work resonating with personal themes, stylistic idiosyncrasies, and the close, confiding tone of one human being addressing another. The posters for their films,

Pedro Almodóvar

When Spain's Fascist government collapsed with the death in 1975 of General Francisco Franco, so did the gray, repressed cinema that his government had sponsored. Suddenly it was time for life, color, and sexuality in Spanish films—a moment that exploded into *Pepi, Luci, Bom* (1980), Almodóvar's first feature and a compendium of the campy delights the Fascists had banned. Almodóvar continued his pursuit of camp through the 1980s, with films like *Law of Desire* (1987) and *Tie Me Up, Tie Me Down* (1989). But his films took a new, mature turn in the 1990s, including *High Heels* (1991) and *All About My Mother* (1999), movies that blended camp comedy and melodramatic excess into an authentic new vision. *Talk to Her*, released in 2002, suggests that Almodóvar has not stopped growing as a filmmaker, as he introduces new notes of melancholy and mortality.

PEDRO ALMODÓVAR
ALL ABOUT MY MOTHER
(*Todo sobre mi madre*)
1999
39 x 27 inches
Spain
Artist/Designer: Óscar Mariné

PEDRO ALMODÓVAR
WOMEN ON THE VERGE OF
A NERVOUS BREAKDOWN
(*Zeny na pokraji*
nervoveho zhrouceni)
1988
16 x 11 inches
Czechoslovakia
Artist/Designer: Weber

SPOUTEJ MĚ !

ŠPANĚLSKÝ FILM

PSYCHOPAT A HVĚZDA PORNOFILMŮ V POUTECH LÁSKY

REŽIE: PEDRO ALMODÓVAR

V HLAVNÍCH ROLÍCH VICTORIA ABRIL
A ANTONIO BANDERAS

Atame!

DISTRIBUTOR
LUCERNAFILM
Beta

Robert Altman

Robert Altman's aggressive antiestablishment stance, indifference to craftsmanship, and acerbic wit have made him the spiritual godfather of an entire school of contemporary independent filmmaking. When *M*A*S*H* became an unexpected critical and commercial success in 1970, it bought Altman almost two decades of credit, during which he turned out a series of highly experimental films—among them *Images*, *The Long Goodbye*, and *McCabe and Mrs. Miller*—that eventually faded out in the debacles of *Popeye* and *O.C. and Stiggs*. But then, on the brink of unbankability, Altman came through with the sleeper hit *The Player*, leading to another series of personal projects, including *Kansas City* and *Dr. T and the Women*.

ROBERT ALTMAN
A WEDDING (Svatba)
1980
33 x 23 inches
Czechoslovakia
Artist/Designer:
Ziegler Design

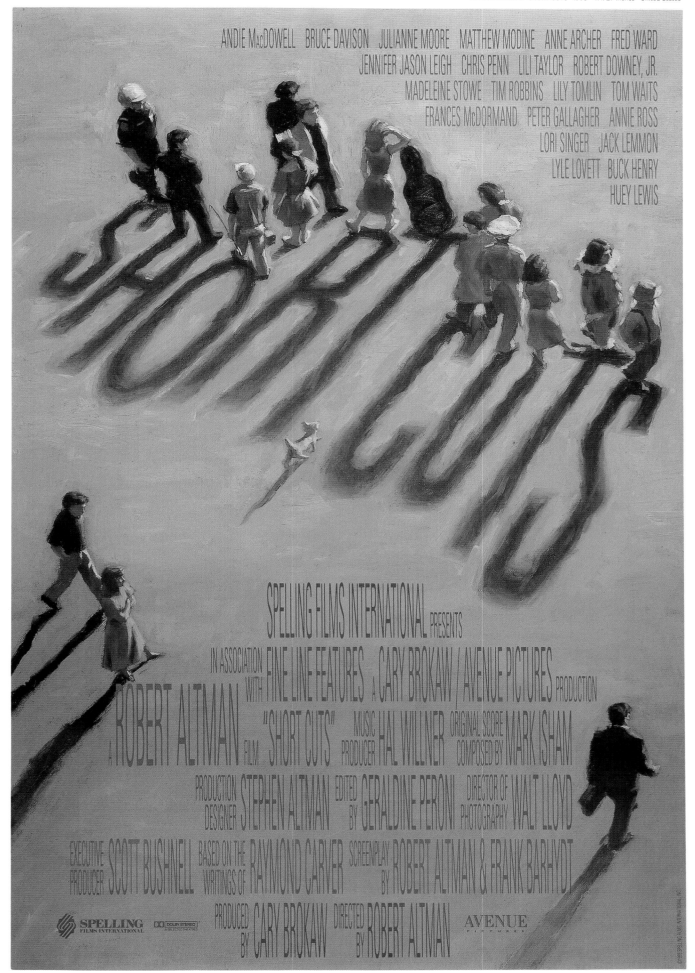

Paul Thomas Anderson

A product of Los Angeles's eternally vilified San Fernando Valley, Anderson has brought an epic sensibility to independent filmmaking with his large, ensemble casts and sociological vision, directed toward such exotic cultures as the pornography industry (*Boogie Nights* [1997]) and the strip-mall suburbs (*Magnolia* [1999]). An uncompromising personal filmmaker, Anderson nevertheless collaborated with the most blatantly commercial of contemporary movie stars, the money machine known as Adam Sandler, on *Punch-Drunk Love* (2002), an eccentric, intimate love story punctuated by evocative if inexplicable poetic moments.

GOLDEN GLOBE
FÜR BURT REYNOLDS

EXCELLENT!
CHICAGO TRIBUNE

**DER HEISSESTE
FILM AMERIKAS**

**TOP FILM
OF THE YEAR**
NATIONAL BOARD OF REVIEW

IT's THE BOMB!
DETROIT FREE PRESS

**ES IST, WIE WENN
»GOODFELLAS«
»PULP FICTION«
TRIFFT**
TIME MAGAZIN

Boogie Nights
···· THE SEVENTIES - UNZIPPED ····

CONSTANTIN FILM und NEW LINE CINEMA präsentieren EINE LAWRENCE GORDON PRODUKTION EIN P.T. ANDERSON FILM »BOOGIE NIGHTS« MARK WAHLBERG JULIANNE MOORE BURT REYNOLDS DON CHEADLE JOHN C. REILLY WILLIAM H. MACY HEATHER GRAHAM NICOLE PARKER PHILLIP SEYMORE HOFFMANN MUSIK MICHAEL PENN KOSTÜME MARK BRIDGES SCHNITT DYLAN TICHENOR AUSSTATTUNG BOB ZIEMBICKI KAMERA ROBERT ELSWIT CO-PRODUZENT DANIEL LUPI AUSFÜHRENDE CO-PRODUZENTEN MICHAEL DE LUCA LYNN HARRIS AUSFÜHRENDER PRODUZENT LAWRENCE GORDON PRODUZENTEN LLOYD LEVIN JOHN LYONS PAUL THOMAS ANDERSON JOANNE SELLAR DREHBUCH UND REGIE PAUL THOMAS ANDERSON

NEW LINE CINEMA ■ DOLBY SR Soundtrack bei EMI erhältlich

Constantin Film

Mehr Informationen über »BOOGIE NIGHTS« und dieses Kino online unter http://www.moviedata.de

Gregg Araki

Emerging from the student film underground with his 1992 *The Living End*, Araki became one of the exemplars of the New Queer Cinema, a movement devoted to forthright and politically provocative images of homosexuality. But where many of his New Queer colleagues floundered in didacticism and endless remakes of the teen coming-out tale, Araki moved on to darker things, creating in *Totally F***ed Up* (1993), a vision of gay bohemia that was anything but utopian and optimistic. Continuing with *The Doom Generation* (1995), Araki has raised discomfiting issues and, in his 1999 effort, *Splendor*, has even flirted with heterosexuality.

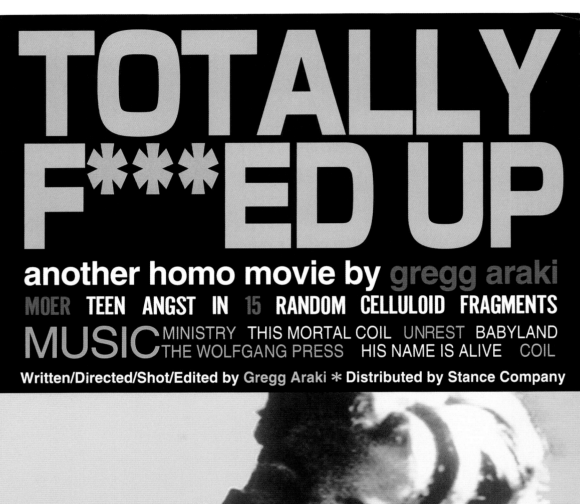

GREGG ARAKI
*TOTALLY F***ED UP*
1994
29 x 20 inches
Japan

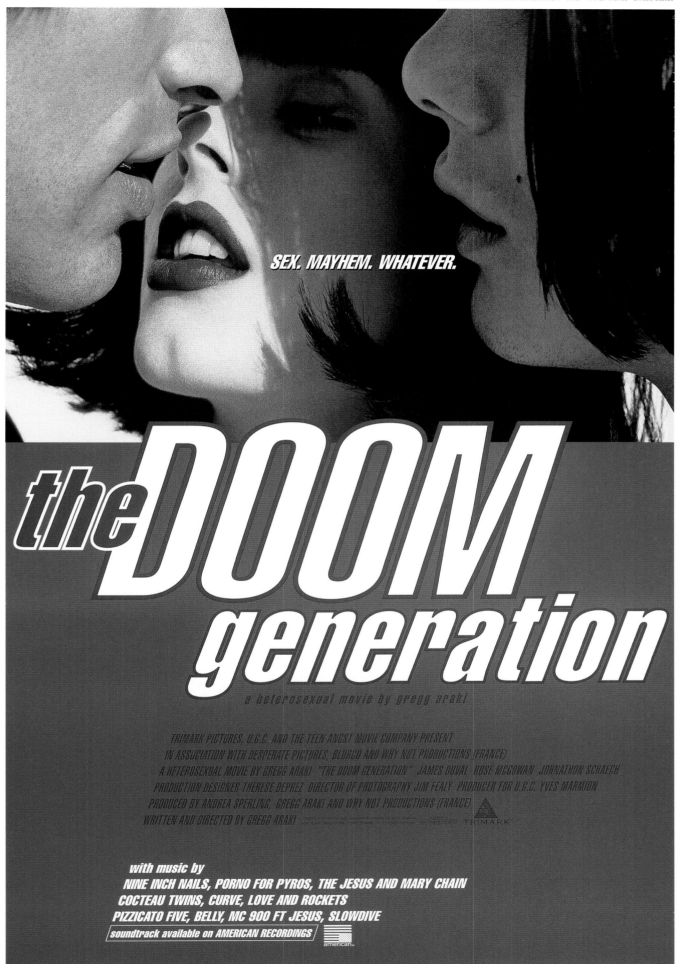

Darren Aronofsky

With his 1998 *Pi*, Brooklyn-born Darren Aronofsky brought a sense of formal experimentation back to an independent film scene that had become centered on scripts and performances. A paranoid thriller filmed in black and white, *Pi* drew on the densely composed images of Fritz Lang (*The Testament of Dr. Mabuse* [1933]) and Orson Welles (particularly *The Trial* [1962]). Aronofsky's second feature, *Requiem for a Dream* (2000) was more conventional in its choice of literary source material (a novel by Hubert Selby, Jr.) and professional cast (Jared Leto, Jennifer Connelly, Ellen Burstyn), but still showed a willingness to break out of conventional psychological realism for more extreme effects.

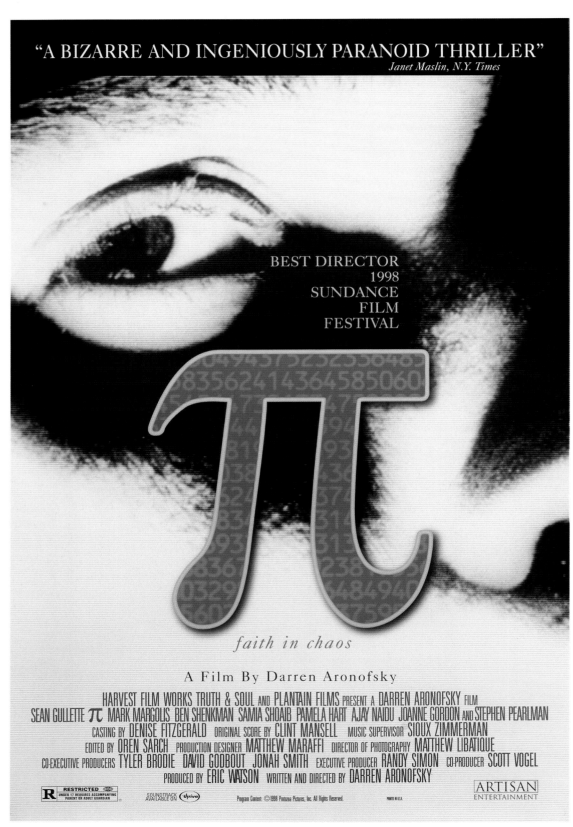

DARREN ARONOFSKY
PI
1998
41 x 27 inches
United States
Artists/Designers:
Darren Aronofsky
Jeremy Dawson
Dan Schrecker
Matthew Libatique

Joel and Ethan Coen

The Coen brothers—Joel, who writes and directs, and Ethan, who writes and produces—had one of the first commercial hits of the emerging indie movement with their comic thriller of 1984, *Blood Simple*. The Coen formula combines breathtaking technical mastery with plot lines that parody genre conventions and play on the audience's ingrained knowledge of what will happen next, the power of which was proved with the considerable commercial success of *Fargo* (1996). The Coens score stronger on attitude and intelligence than they do on heart and substance, but their cynical sensibility has proven a handy counterweight to the often painful earnestness of much independent filmmaking.

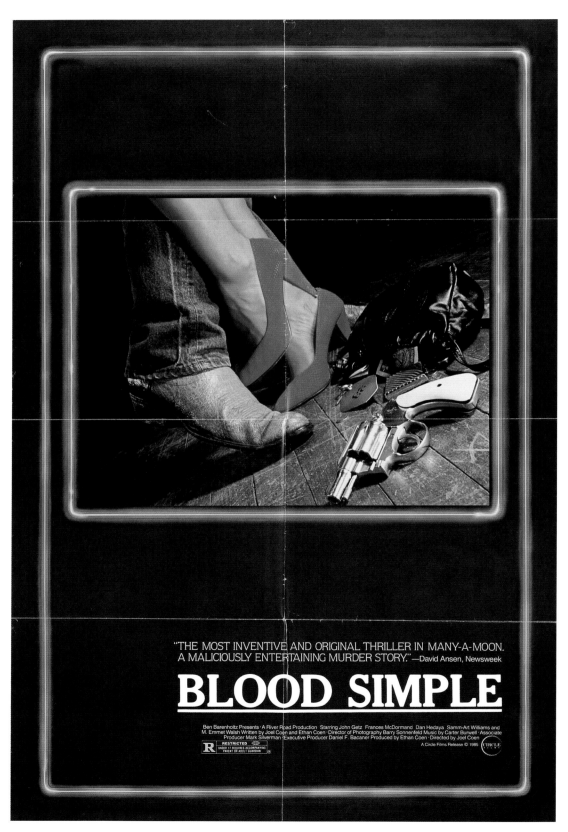

JOEL AND ETHAN COEN
BLOOD SIMPLE
1984
41 x 27 inches
United States

Alex Cox

British-born, UCLA-educated Alex Cox combines a Marxist take on social injustice with a flair for absurdist comedy. His 1986 *Sid and Nancy*, about the self-doomed punk rocker Sid Vicious and his braying American girlfriend, Nancy Spungen, remains a classic of rock-and-roll romantic nihilism as well as his best-known film. Though Cox has continued to experiment and provoke—as with the faux spaghetti-Western *Straight to Hell* (1988) and the politically pointed *Walker* (1988), he has been unable to find an accommodating home base either in Europe or America, and his reputation has slipped as his activity has diminished.

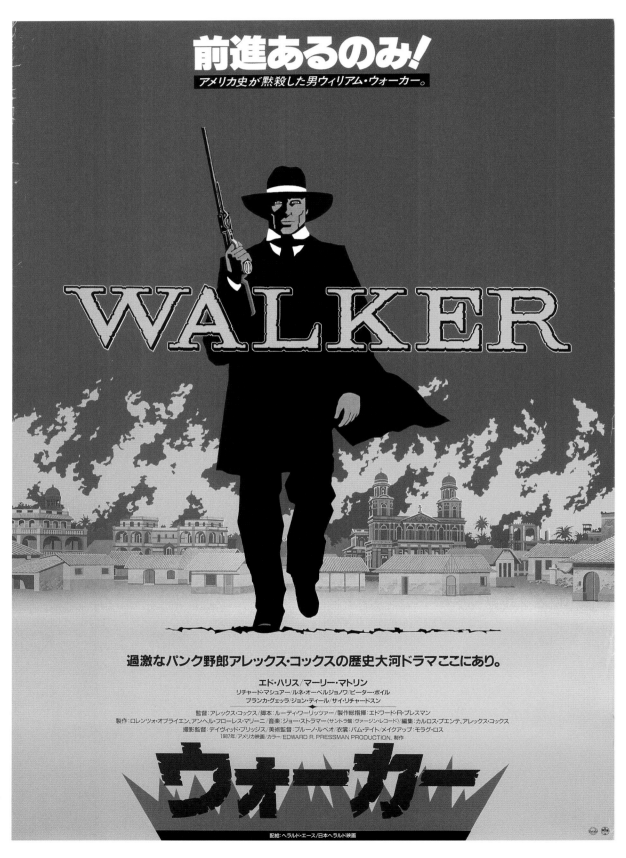

ALEX COX
WALKER
1988
29 x 20 inches
Japan

David Cronenberg

A product of that "other" independent cinema—the one that fills double-bills at drive-ins and inner-city theaters—Cronenberg has advanced from disreputable shockers with titles like *They Came from Within* (1975) and *Rabid* (1977) to high-toned literary projects such as *Naked Lunch* (1990, from the novel by William S. Burroughs) and *Spider* (2002, from the novel by Patrick McGrath). But Cronenberg's perverse, poetic sensibility has only deepened with time. Where once he used horror metaphors to describe his notion of the human body as a malleable machine that could be reshaped by technology and emotion, he now works out his ideas in less extreme images, concentrating the metaphysical disgust of *Spider*, for example, in bizarrely cramped spaces and brackish colors.

DAVID CRONENBERG
NAKED LUNCH
1990
41 x 27 inches
United States

DAVID CRONENBERG
NAKED LUNCH
1990
29 x 20 inches
Japan
Artist/Designer: Hajime Sorayama

DAVID CRONENBERG
SPIDER
2002
29 x 20 inches
Japan

John Dahl

A reliable maker of modest thrillers, such as 1989's *Kill Me Again* and 1993's *Red Rock West*, John Dahl broke into new ground with *The Last Seduction* in 1994–a classic, straight-faced film noir that offered a femme fatale for the post-feminist era in the frightening figure of Linda Fiorentino as a manipulative wife. Hollywood has not since been kind to Dahl's reserved, classical talents, saddling him with half-finished scripts (*Unforgettable* [1996]) and callow casts (*Joy Ride* [2001]). He has both too much personality and too little commercial clout to function happily in the new, brutally pragmatic studio climate.

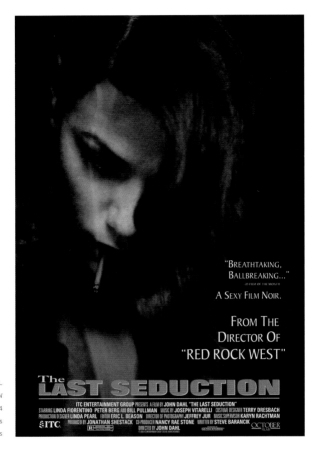

JOHN DAHL
THE LAST SEDUCTION
1994
41 x 27 inches
United States

JOHN DAHL
RED ROCK WEST
1993
30 x 40 inches
Great Britain

Jean-Luc Godard

An independent among independents, Jean-Luc Godard has made a career of questioning the fundamentals of his medium, from the deconstructed genre films of his early period (*Breathless* [1960]; *A Woman Is a Woman* [1961]), to the sometimes frustrating, always beautiful essay films of his later years. With *Passion* (1982), Godard began exploring the differences between film and video and the distinct manners in which they capture reality. He has continued this theme through the difficult but visually ravishing *In Praise of Love* (2001), which perversely but appropriately uses video to depict the past and film to depict the present.

JEAN-LUC GODARD *KEEP UP YOUR RIGHT (Soigne ta droite)* 1988 40 x 25 inches Switzerland Artist/Designer: Paul Brühwiler

1954 «Opération Beton»
1955 «Une femme coquette»
1957 «Tous les garçons s'appellent
       Patrick»
       (ou «Charlotte et Véronique»)
1958 «Charlotte et son Jules»
       «Une histoire d'Eau»
1959 «A bout de souffle»
1960 «Le petit soldat»
1961 «Une femme est une femme»
       «La paresse»
1962 «Vivre sa vie»
       «Le nouveau monde»
1963 «Les carabiniers»
       «Le grand escroc»
       «Le mépris»
1964 «Montparnasse-Levallois»
       «Bande à part»
       «Une femme mariée»
1965 «Alphaville»
       «Pierrot le fou»
1966 «Masculin–Féminin»
       «Made in U.S.A.»
       «Deux ou trois choses
       que je sais d'elle»
       «Anticipation»
       (ou «L'Amour en l'an 2000»)
1967 «Loin du Vietnam»

       «La Chinoise»
       «La Contestation»
       «Week End»
1968 «Le gai savoir»
       «Un film comme les autres»
       «One plus one»
       «One American movie»
1969 «British sounds»
       «Pravda»
       «Vent d'Est»
       «Luttes en Italie»
1970 «Jusqu'à la victoire»
1971 «Vladimir et Rosa»
1972 «Tout va bien»
       «Letter to Jane (USA)»
1974 «Ici et ailleurs»
1975 «Numéro deux»
       «Comment ça va»
1976 «Six fois deux»
1978 «France-Tour-Detour-Deux Enfants»
1980 «Sauve qui peut»
1981 «Lettre à Freddy Buache»
1982 «Passion»
1983 «Prénom Carmen»
1985 «Je vous salue Marie»
       «Détective»
1987 «King Lear»
1988 «Soigne ta droite»

SOIGNE TA DROITE

Jean-Luc Godard, né en 1930 à Paris.
Ecole à Nyon: Etudes d'ethnologie à la
Sorbonne. Critique de film pour la Gazette
du cinéma en 1950, à partir du 1952 il écrit
pour le cahier du cinéma. Il tourne son
premier film en 1954

Soigne ta droite. «Soigne ta droite» est
une formule jetée comme une sorte
de masque recouvrant l'un des titres
possibles de ce film, qui ne coïncide pas
avec celui que Godard, jouant le rôle de
l'Idiot, déclare souhaiter tourner et qui
s'intitulerait «Une place sur la terre comme
au ciel»; son action, dispersée en sketches-
fabliaux qui s'emboîtent ou se déboîtent,
s'y développe en zig-zag entre l'azur et le
sol, entre le silence et le chant.

Print & ed / Arts council of Switzerland, PRO HELVETIA
P.O. Box / CH-8024 Zurich, phone: +41/1/221.95.90, FAX: +41/1/201.06.00
Design by Paul Brühwiler, © 1990 by PRO HELVETIA

A film by
JEAN-LUC GODARD

PASSION (15)

ISABELLE HUPPERT
HANNA SCHYGULLA
MICHEL PICCOLI
JERZY RADZIWILOWICZ

PHOTOGRAPHY: RAOUL COUTARD
MUSIC: MOZART · DVORAK · BEETHOVEN · FAURE · RAVEL
SARA FILMS · SONIMAGE · FILMS A2 · FILM ET VIDEO PRODUCTIONS · SSR
SWITZERLAND/FRANCE 1982 SUBTITLE EASTMANCOLOUR

An Artificial Eye Release

JEAN-LUC GODARD   PASSION   1982   30 x 40 inches   Great Britain

Peter Greenaway

Coming from a fine art background, Peter Greenaway has always paid scrupulous attention to the graphic quality of his films and of his promotional material. An adept player of intellectual games, Greenaway usually contrasts the human quest for order (the numbering of the world!) and the equally human addiction to sexual passion and chaos. His themes are probably best elucidated in his first commercial feature, *The Draughtsman's Contract* (1982). As the shock value of his movies, which often contain extensive middle-aged nudity, has diminished, so have his audience and his budget. His later films, such as *The Pillow Book* (1996) and *8 1/2 Women* (1999), suffer from the lack of means to realize his extravagant visions.

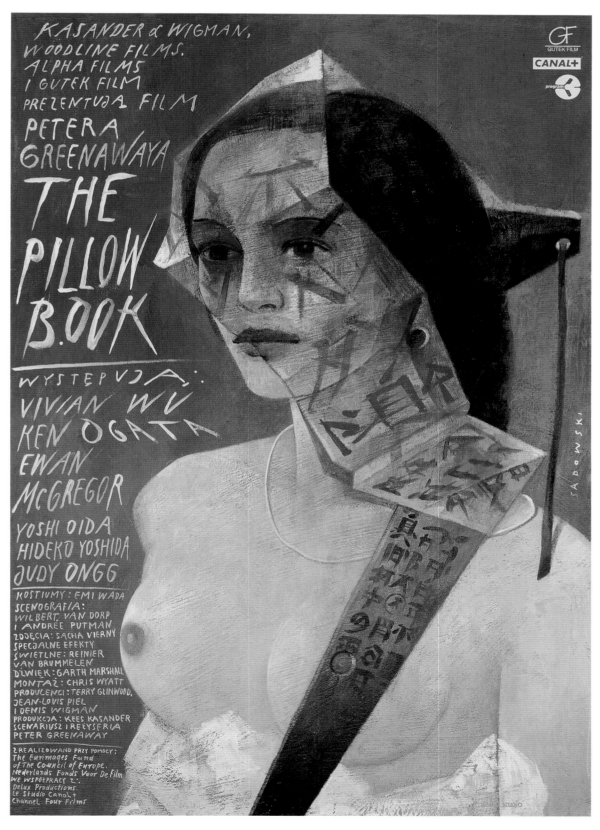

PETER GREENAWAY

THE PILLOW BOOK

1996

38 x 26 inches

Poland

Artist/Designer:

Wiktor Sadowski

PETER GREENAWAY *A ZED AND TWO NOUGHTS* 1985 30 x 40 inches Great Britain

From the director of the internationally acclaimed film THE DRAUGHTSMAN'S CONTRACT

BFI PRODUCTION presents A Peter Greenaway Film

A ZED & TWO NOUGHTS

15

Starring Andrea Ferréol · Brian Deacon · Eric Deacon · Frances Barber · Joss Ackland

Written and Directed by PETER GREENAWAY · Music by MICHAEL NYMAN

Director of Photography SACHA VIERNY · Film Editor JOHN WILSON · Production Designers BEN VAN OS & JAN ROELFS · Producers PETER SAINSBURY & KEES KASANDER
A BFI Production/Allarts Enterprises/Artificial Eye Productions/Film Four International Co-production · Colour · An Artificial Eye Release · Fully illustrated Script Published by Faber & Faber · Original Soundtrack on TER Records and Tapes.

FROM THURS 5th DEC Lumière Cinema ST MARTINS LANE, COVENT GARDEN
TELEPHONE 379 3014 & 836 0691

PETER GREENAWAY *THE DRAUGHTSMAN'S CONTRACT* 1982 30 x 40 inches Great Britain

The Draughtsman's Contract AA
A · F I L M · B Y · P E T E R · G R E E N A W A Y

Written & Directed by PETER GREENAWAY   Photography CURTIS CLARK   Art Direction BOB RINGWOOD   Costumes SUE BLANE   Music MICHAEL NYMAN   A BRITISH FILM INSTITUTE PRODUCTION made in association with CHANNEL 4

PETER GREENAWAY
8 1/2 WOMEN
1999
29 x 20 inches
Japan

PETER GREENAWAY
DROWNING BY NUMBERS
1987
20 x 15 inches
France
Artist/Designer: Benjamin Baltimore

Hal Hartley

Hal Hartley became one of the early stars of the American independent movement with his whimsical fables of suburban romance, *The Unbelievable Truth* (1989) and *Trust* (1991). The 1992 *Simple Men* complicated Hartley's formula with deliberate paradoxes—the film is about two brothers, one a professional thief, the other a meek philosophy student—and a baffling thriller subplot. Ambition surpassed accomplishment with *Henry Fool* (1998), and Hartley has not recaptured the light-hearted, self-deprecating tone that redeemed his early work, plunging instead into the mythological pomposity of *No Such Thing* (2001). Still, he is one of the few indie directors to build his own stable of stars, including Martin Donovan, Adrienne Shelly, and Robert Burke.

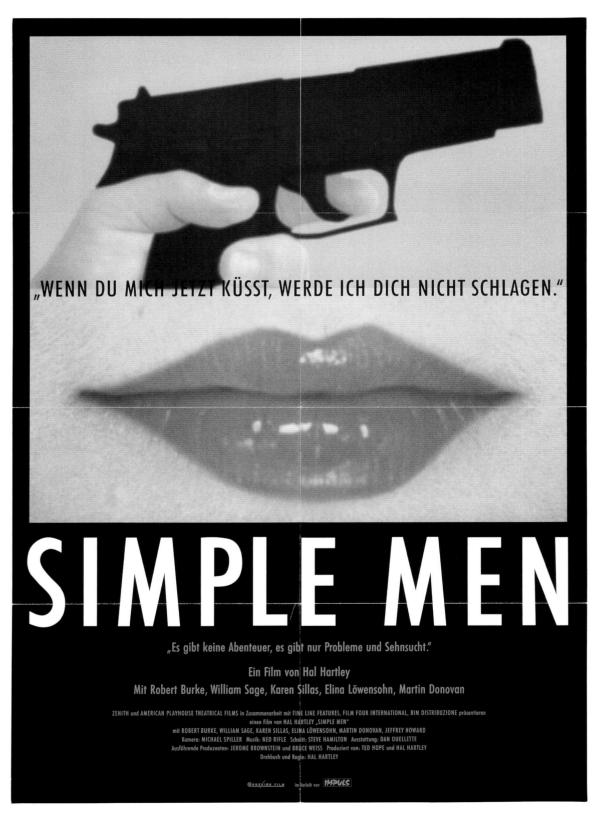

HAL HARTLEY
SIMPLE MEN
1992
32 x 23 inches
Germany

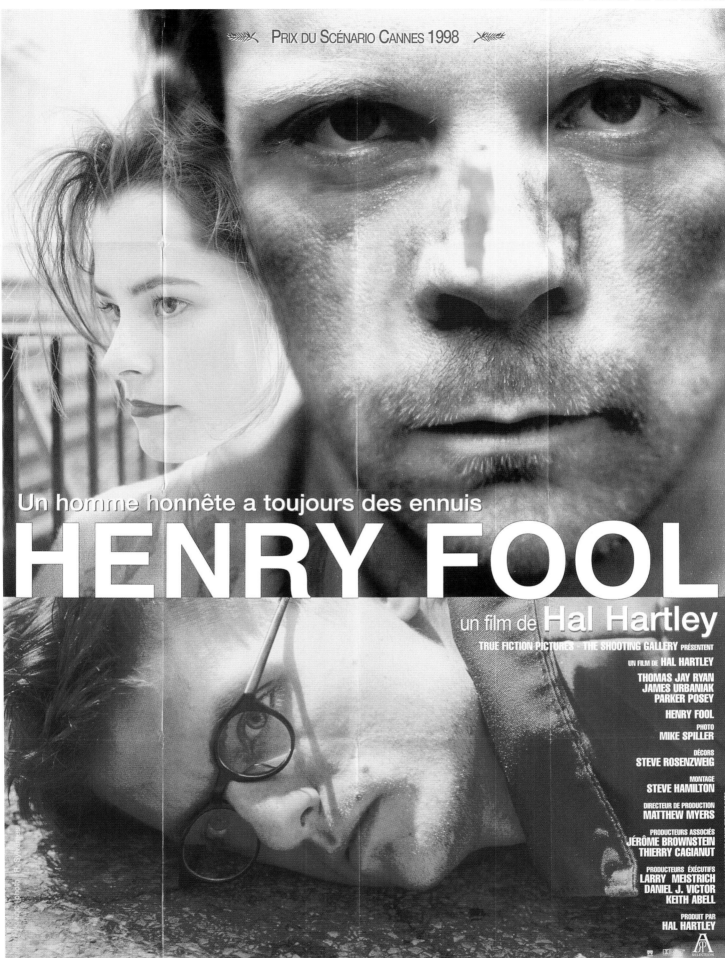

Todd Haynes

It's ironic that Todd Haynes has become known for the beauty and accuracy of his low-budget period re-creations—of the 1970s in *Velvet Goldmine* (1998) and the 1950s in *Far from Heaven* (2002). His real gift is for structural experimentation—the scrambling of styles and genres in his debut feature *Poison* (1991), or the Antonioni-like silences and enigmas of 1995's *Safe*. No mere set decorator, Haynes is focused on that peculiar American determinism that says appearance is fate.

TODD HAYNES
POISON
1991
41 x 27 inches
United States
Artist/Designer:
Todd Haynes
(Concepts and
sketches)

Jim Jarmusch

Like Alfred Hitchcock, Jim Jarmusch has succeeded in making his own face more recognizable than many of his actors. With *Stranger Than Paradise* (1984) and *Down by Law* (1986), Jarmusch established an immediately identifiable visual style, defined by a standoffish, unmoving camera, stark black-and-white compositions, and very little movement within shots. At his best, Jarmusch transforms his visual stasis into rich character comedy, as his retiring heroes—often foreigners desperately out of their element—search for happiness amid the utter indifference of their surroundings, as the couples of *Mystery Train* (1989) strive to do in the streets of Memphis. The danger for Jarmusch is that his method can freeze into formula, as it does in the criminally unambitious *Ghost Dog* (1999).

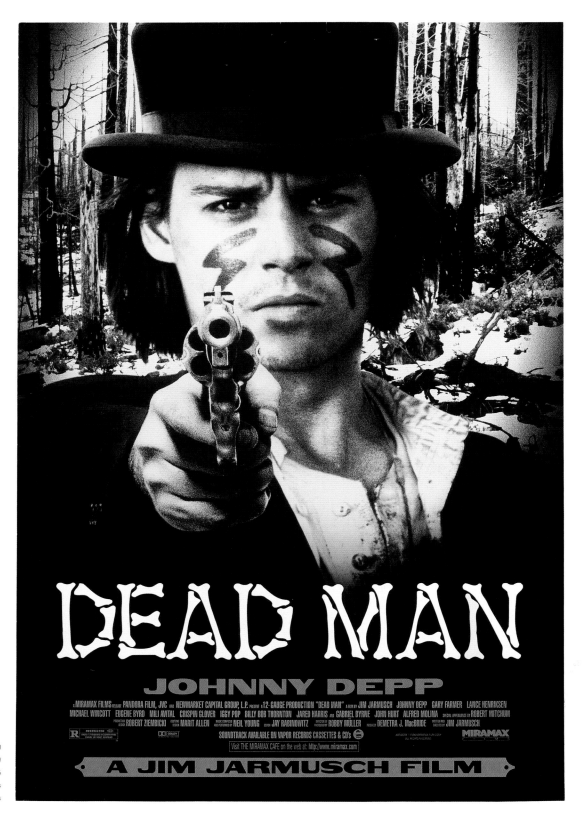

JIM JARMUSCH
DEAD MAN
1996
41 x 27 inches
United States

POZA PRAWEM DOWN BY LAW

scenariusz i reżyseria: JIM JARMUSCH   zdjęcia: ROBBY MÜLLER   muzyka: JOHN LURIE

wykonawcy: TOM WAITS, JOHN LURIE, ROBERTO BENIGNI piosenki: TOM WAITSproducent: ALAN KLEINBERG

szefowie produkcji: OTTO GROKENBERGER, CARY BROKAW, RUSSELL SCHWARTZ koproducenci: TOM ROTHMAN, JIM STARK

produkcja: A BLACK SNAKE/GROKENBERGER FILM - 1986

VISUAL STUDIO WARSAW — POLAND — Tel. (02) 642-22-35

59

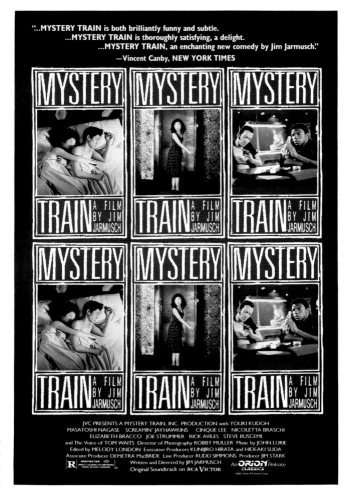

JIM JARMUSCH
MYSTERY TRAIN
1989
41 x 27 inches
United States

JIM JARMUSCH
MYSTERY TRAIN
1991
38 x 26 inches
Poland
Artist/Designer:
Andrzej Klimowski

NOC NA ZIEMI film JIMA JARMUSCHA

night on earth

muzyka TOM WAITS
produkcja JVC–LOCUS SOLUS

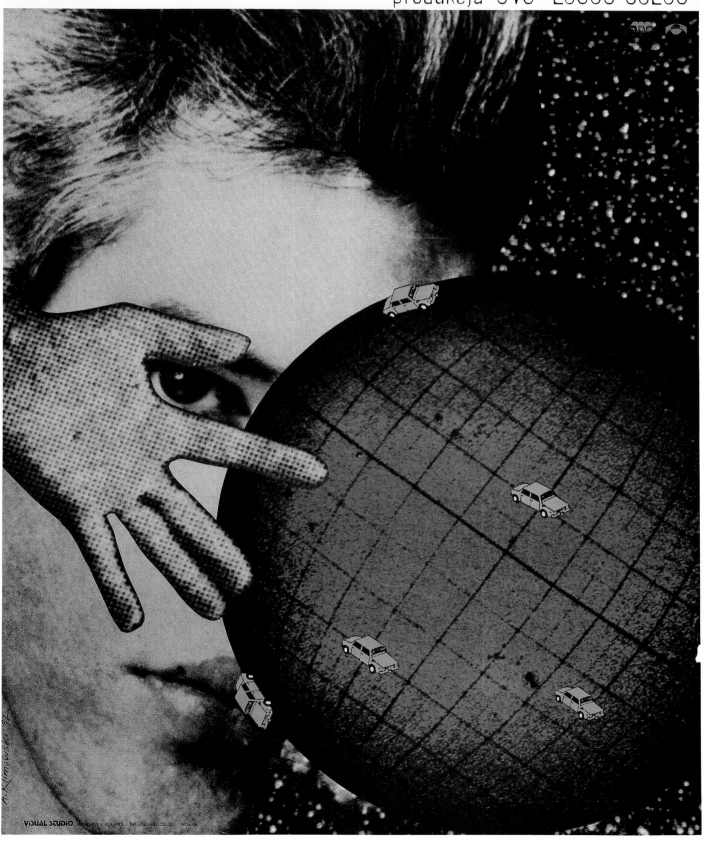

JIM JARMUSCH

GHOST DOG

1999

20 x 15 inches

France

STRANGER THAN PARADISE
A NEW AMERICAN FILM

"An enchanting film...made with heart and wit. It doesn't
feel quite like any other movie you've seen before."
Roger Ebert, Chicago Sun-Times

JIM JARMUSCH

STRANGER THAN PARADISE

1984

41 x 27 inches

United States

THE SAMUEL GOLDWYN COMPANY PRESENTS A FILM BY JIM JARMUSCH
WITH **JOHN LURIE** **ESZTER BALINT** **RICHARD EDSON**
EXECUTIVE PRODUCER/OTTO GROKENBERGER PRODUCER/SARA DRIVER
MUSIC/JOHN LURIE WRITER-DIRECTOR/JIM JARMUSCH

INACZEJ NIZ W RAJU

STRANGER THAN PARADISE

scenariusz i reżyseria: JIM JARMUSCH
wykonawcy: JOHN LURIE, ESZTER BALINT, RICHARD EDSON
zdjęcia: THOMAS DICILLO muzyka: JOHN LURIE producent: SARA DRIVER
ZŁOTY LEOPARD - LOCARNO 1984 - ZŁOTA KAMERA - CANNES 1984

produkcja: GROKENBERGER FILM - Monachium CINESTHESIA PRODUCTIONS INC. - Nowy Jork oraz ZDF - 1984

A. Klimowski '91

VISUAL STUDIO WARSAW POLAND · Tel (02) 642 22 35

Jean-Pierre Jeunet and Marc Caro

Though they have since gone their separate ways (Jeunet to direct the international hit *Amélie* [2001], Caro to a career as a production designer), the team produced two of the oddest films to come out of France in the 1990s–the elaborately constructed black comedy *Delicatessen* (1991), and the dark children's tale *The City of Lost Children* (1995). Going against the French cinema's traditional focus on psychological realism and photographic naturalism, Jeunet and Caro dragged Gallic film, kicking and screaming, into the abstract, anything-goes world of sophisticated special effects.

JEAN-PIERRE JEUNET,
MARC CARO
DELICATESSEN
1991
33 x 23 inches
Czech Republic

LUMIERE, LE STUDIO CANAL +, FRANCE 3 CINEMA présentent une production CLAUDIE OSSARD

La Cité
des Enfants Perdus

Un film de JEUNET & CARO

Avec RON PERLMAN · Daniel EMILFORK · Judith VITTET · Dominique PINON · Jean-Claude DREYFUS · Geneviève BRUNET · Odile MALLET · Mireille MOSSE · Serge MERLIN
François HADJI-LAZARO · RUFUS · Ticky HOLGADO · et la participation de Jean-Louis TRINTIGNANT
Scénario de Gilles ADRIEN, Jean-Pierre JEUNET, Marc CARO · Dialogues de Gilles ADRIEN · Musique originale d'Angelo BADALAMENTI · Directeur de la photographie : Darius KHONDJI (AFC) · Décor : Jean RABASSE
Costumes : Jean-Paul GAULTIER · Son : Pierre EXCOFFIER · Montage : Hervé SCHNEID · Montage son : Gérard HARDY · Mixage : Vincent ARNARDI et Thierry LEBON · Effets spéciaux numériques : PITOF · Images de synthèse : Pierre BUFFIN
Directeur de production : Daniel SZUSTER · Produit par Claudie OSSARD une coproduction CONSTELLATION, LUMIERE, LE STUDIO CANAL +, FRANCE 3 CINEMA
Avec la participation du Centre National de la Cinématographie, de Cofimage 4, Cofimage 5, Studio Image Canal +, et le soutien de la Procirep. Coproducteurs européens : Elias Querejeta (Espagne) et Tele Munchen (Allemagne)
Avec le soutien du Fonds Eurimages du Conseil de L'Europe et la collaboration du Club d'Investissement Média (Programme Média de l'Union Européenne)

DOLBY STEREO DIGITAL

Bande originale du film disponible sur CD et K7 - EAST WEST

UGC

Aki Kaurismäki

Finland's leading filmmaker—his only real competition is his older brother, Mika—Aki Kaurismäki is the reigning master of deadpan comic despair, chronicling the lives of hopeless losers and congenital misfits with a wit and compassion that seem to deepen with each new film. Whether he is imagining the misadventures of a so-square-they're-hip rock band, the Leningrad Cowboys, on their desultory tour of backwater American bars (*Leningrad Cowboys Go America* [1988]), or the love life of an unemployed mineworker (*Ariel* [1989]), Kaurismäki is the poet of the perfectly banal, wrenching humor and emotion from the most oppressively ordinary of situations.

AKI KAURISMÄKI
*LENINGRAD COWBOYS
GO AMERICA*
(*Leningrad Cowboys
jada do Ameryki*)
1989
38 x 26 inches
Poland
Artist/Designer:
Waldemar Swierzy

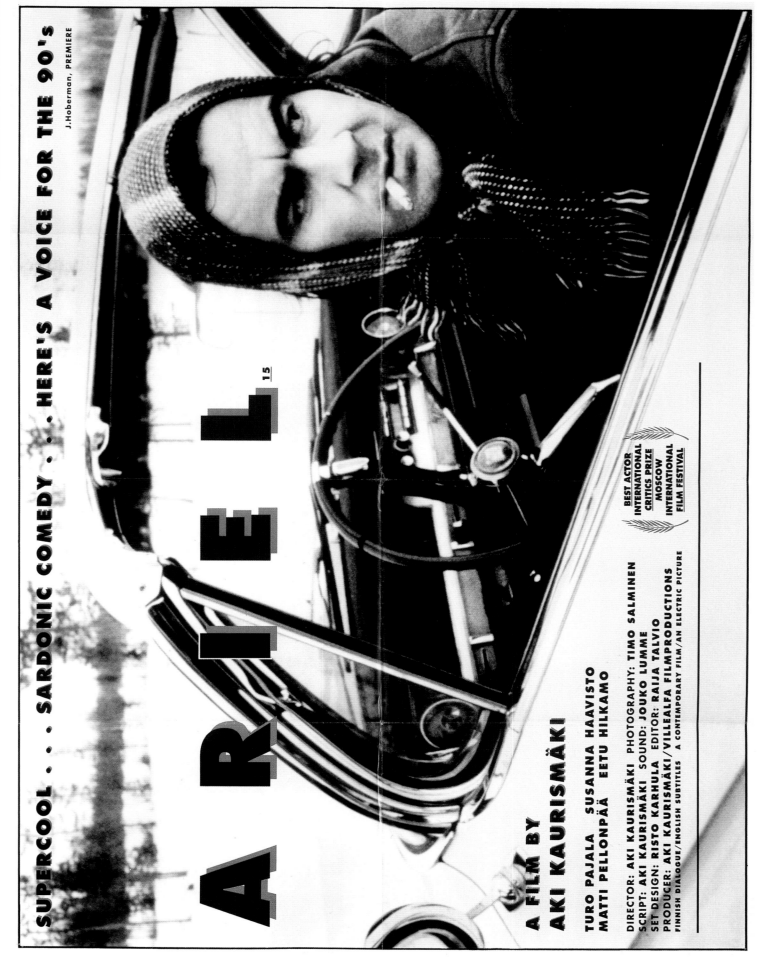

SUPERCOOL . . . . SARDONIC COMEDY . . . HERE'S A VOICE FOR THE 90's

J.Hoberman, PREMIERE

ARIEL 15

BEST ACTOR
INTERNATIONAL
CRITICS PRIZE
MOSCOW
INTERNATIONAL
FILM FESTIVAL

A FILM BY AKI KAURISMÄKI

TURO PAJALA   SUSANNA HAAVISTO
MATTI PELLONPÄÄ   EETU HILKAMO

DIRECTOR: AKI KAURISMÄKI PHOTOGRAPHY: TIMO SALMINEN
SCRIPT: AKI KAURISMÄKI SOUND: JOUKO LUMME
SET DESIGN: RISTO KARHULA EDITOR: RAIJA TALVIO
PRODUCER: AKI KAURISMÄKI/VILLEALFA FILMPRODUCTIONS
FINNISH DIALOGUE/ENGLISH SUBTITLES   A CONTEMPORARY FILM/AN ELECTRIC PICTURE

Krzysztof Kieslowski

Poland's Krzysztof Kieslowski developed his sense of independence when it was politically and physically dangerous to do so: under a Communist government that tolerated no open dissent. After making a number of provocative documentaries, Kieslowski made his feature-length fiction debut with *Camera Buff* (1979), a thinly veiled allegory about the freedom of expression in his home country. His best-known work remains *The Decalogue*, a ten-part series created for Polish television in 1988, in which each of the Ten Commandments is considered in a context that brings out the ambiguity in their apparently straightforward dictates. *A Short Film About Killing* (1988) and *A Short Film About Love* (1988) are feature-length expansions of *The Decalogue* episodes, designed to stand on their own.

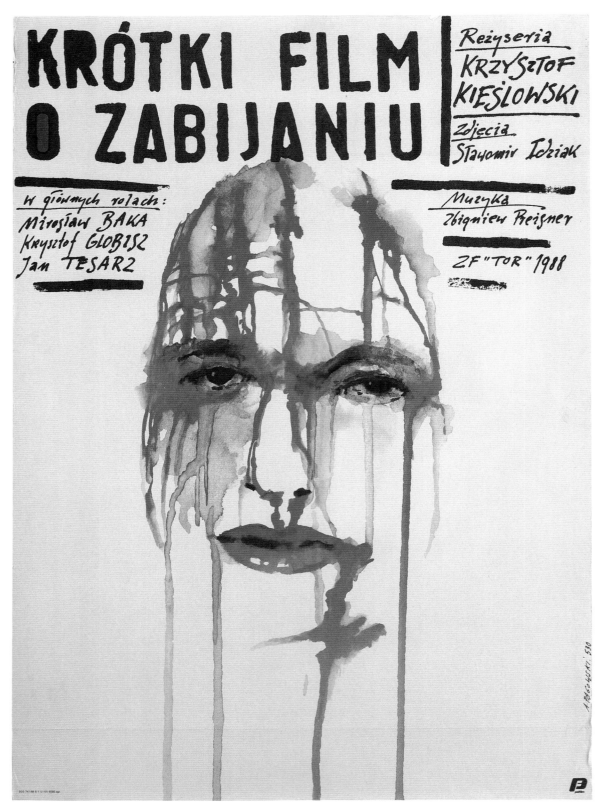

KRZYSZTOF KIESLOWSKI
*A SHORT FILM
ABOUT KILLING*
(Krótki film o zabijaniu)
1988
39 x 27 inches
Poland
Artist/Designer:
Andrzej Pagowski

Takeshi "Beat" Kitano

One of Japan's most popular and hardest-working television personalities (as a performer, he's billed as "Beat" Kitano), Takeshi Kitano opened an unlikely sideline as a maker of extremely violent films noirs in the 1990s, beginning with the startling *Violent Cop* (1989), a project he took over from the veteran Japanese action director Kinji Fukusaku. Kitano's work has since evolved toward a delicate balance of gut-wrenching violence and delicate sentiment, perhaps best represented by his *Hana-bi* (*Fireworks*) of 1997.

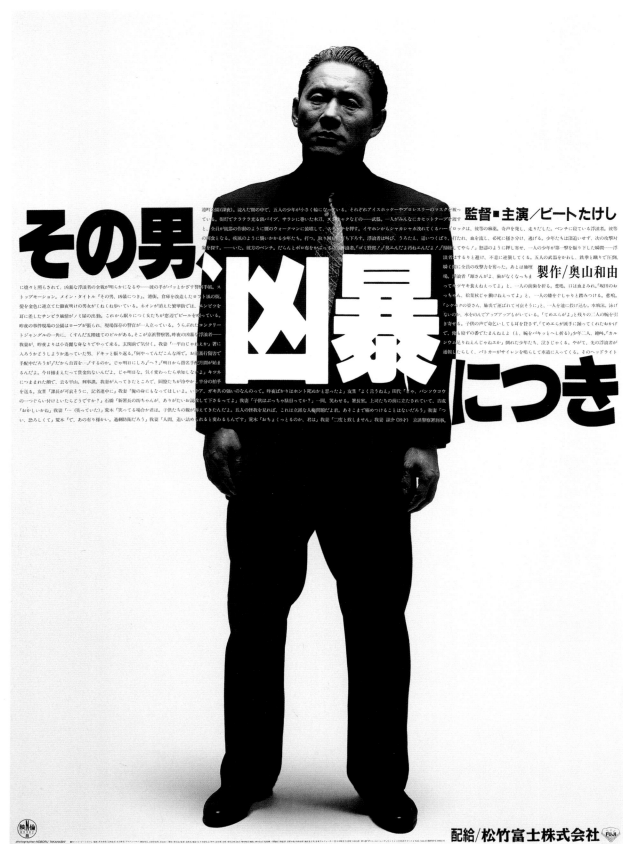

その時に 抱きとめてくれるひとがいますか

北野武監督作品

A FILM Directed By Takeshi Kitano

BEAT Takeshi Kayoko KISHIMOTO Ren OSUGI Susumu TERAJIMA

HANA-BI

Written by Takeshi KITANO Music by Joe Hisaishi

BANDAI VISUAL, TELEVISION TOKYO CHANNEL 12, TOKYO FM and OFFICE KITANO PRESENT

第54回ベネチア国際映画祭金獅子賞受賞

ビートたけし 岸本加世子 大杉漣 寺島進

脚本:北野武 音楽監督:久石譲

製作:バンダイビジュアル・テレビ東京・TOKYO FM/オフィス北野 配給:オフィス北野・日本ヘラルド映画 プロデューサー:森昌行・柘植靖司・吉田多喜男
協力プロデューサー:石川博・古川一博 撮影:山本英夫 照明:高屋齋 美術:磯田典宏 録音:堀内戦治 編集:北野武・太田義彦 記録:中田秀子 助監督:清水浩 キャスティング:吉川威史 製作:小宮慎二 製作管理:山崎義人

[URL] http://www.trans.or.jp/OFFICE-KITANO

Harmony Korine

With only two features–*Gummo* (1997) and *Julien Donkey-Boy* (1999)–to his credit (as well as the screen-play for Larry Clark's notorious *Kids* [1995]), Korine is one of the most controversial figures in American independent cinema, a restless provocateur whose take on adolescent angst suggests *Rebel Without a Cause* (1955) crossed with *Mondo Cane* (1962). A pioneer of digital video filmmaking, Korine uses the intimacy and technical imperfections of the medium to his great advantage, creating films that are at once convincingly real in their social observations and thoroughly dreamlike in their delirious subjectivity.

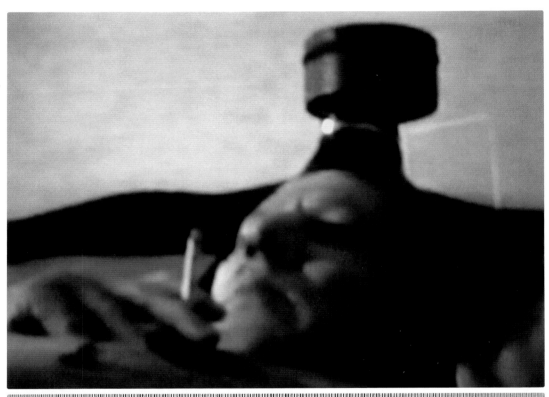

julien donkey-boy

from the award-winning creator of kids and gummo
a film by harmony korine
official selection new york film festival
screening wednesday, september 29, 9pm - alice tully hall (lincoln center)
thursday, september 30, 6pm - alice tully hall (lincoln center)
coming to the angelika film center october 8

HARMONY KORINE
JULIEN DONKEY-BOY
1999
36 x 24 inches
United States
Artist/Designer:
Richard Pandiscio

From the creator of KIDS

FiNE LiNE FEATURES PRESENTS AN INDEPENDENT PiCTURES PRODUCTION OF A HARMONY KORiNE FILM GUMMO
LiNDA MANZ MAX PERLiCH JACOB REYNOLDS CHLOE SEViGNY JACOB SEWELL NiCK SUTTON
COSTUME DESIGNER CHLOE SEViGNY PRODUCTION DESIGNER DAVE DOERNBERG MUSIC SUPERVISOR RANDALL POSTER
EDITOR CHRISTOPHER TELLEFSEN DIRECTOR OF PHOTOGRAPHY JEAN YVES ESCOFFiER
CO-PRODUCERS ROBiN O'HARA AND SCOTT MACAULAY EXECUTIVE PRODUCERS RUTH ViTALE STEPHEN CHiN
PRODUCED BY CARY WOODS WRITTEN AND DIRECTED BY HARMONY KORiNE

 SOUNDTRACK AVAILABLE ON LONDON CDS DOLBY IN SELECTED THEATRES Independent Pictures © 1997 FINE LINE FEATURES. ALL RIGHTS RESERVED.   FiNE LiNE FEATURES A division of New Line Cinema

Visit the Fine Line Features web site at www.flf.com

73

Spike Lee

Melvin Van Peebles's 1971 *Sweet Sweetback's Baadasssss Song* demonstrated that independent filmmaking could give African Americans a voice they seldom had under the studio system, and Spike Lee has followed in that tradition. *She's Gotta Have It* (1986) discarded Hollywood clichés of ghetto life in favor of a sharp, contemporary view of the romantic difficulties of the black bourgeoisie, and incidentally launched Lee (who also acts in many of his films) as a reliably voluble media figure. The 1997 HBO documentary *4 Little Girls* (1997) is Lee's look back at the civil rights movement of the 1960s, through the ghostly figures of children killed in a racist church bombing. His least aggressively stylish film, it may also be his most moving.

SPIKE LEE
4 LITTLE GIRLS
1997
36 x 24 inches
United States

Mike Leigh

The British director Mike Leigh owes the extraordinary emotional textures of his films—such as the family drama *Life Is Sweet* (1991) and the urban angst-fest *Naked* (1993)—to his unique process of developing a screenplay through intense improvisatory sessions with his actors, who in a sense become the authors of their own roles. Unlike so many of his English colleagues, Leigh has resisted the period film as a means of conquering international markets (though his life of Gilbert and Sullivan, *Topsy-Turvy* [1999], was a significant exception). His settings are not country houses, but estate housing—the UK equivalent of American housing projects. Leigh's films about working- and lower-middle-class Britons have no equivalent in the American independent cinema, which remains devoted to romanticized farmers and youthful bohemians.

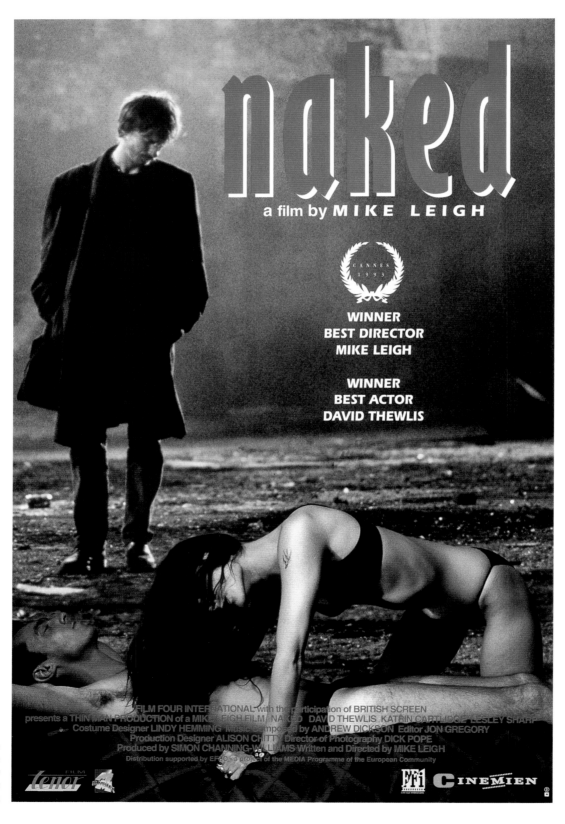

MIKE LEIGH
NAKED
1993
24 x 16 inches
Belgium

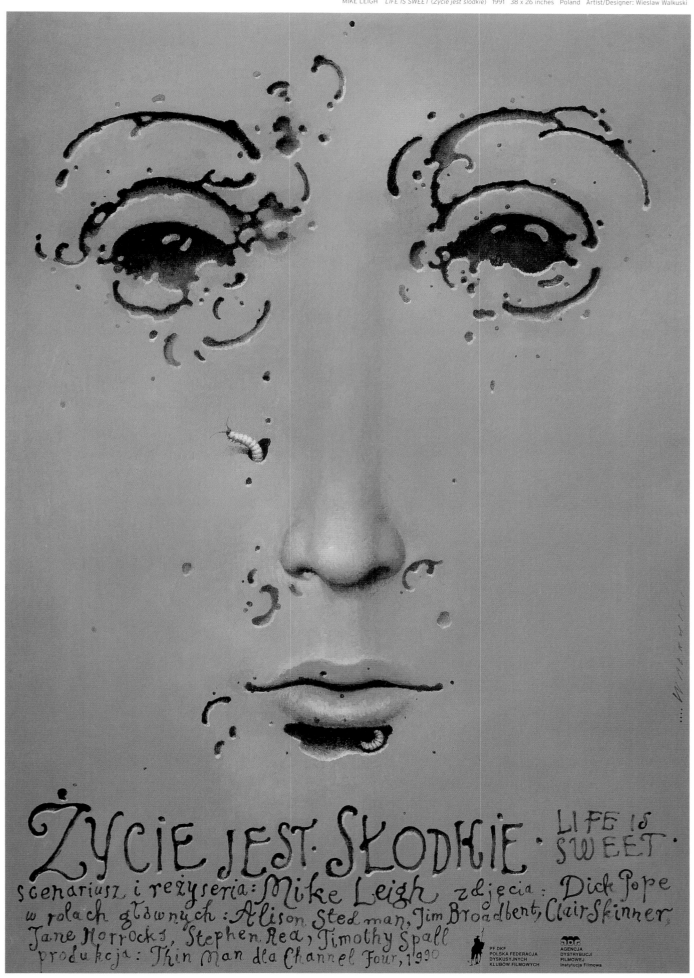

Richard Linklater

The title of Richard Linklater's 1991 *Slacker* added a new word to the English language, meaning those aimless overaged American adolescents who eke out a mysterious existence in the no-man's land between graduation from college and gainful employment. Just as Linklater's camera seemed to glide through the Austin, Texas, of *Slacker*, randomly choosing the individuals who would become its characters, so has Linklater made drifting part of his style. In *Dazed and Confused* (1993), it is substance abuse that links the characters, more than any predefined plot. Both *Before Sunrise* (1995) and its 2004 sequel, *Before Sunset*, are structured as casual tours of an urban landscape, the character relationships developing as they drift toward a destination that neither of them know.

RICHARD LINKLATER

SLACKER

1991

41 x 27 inches

United States

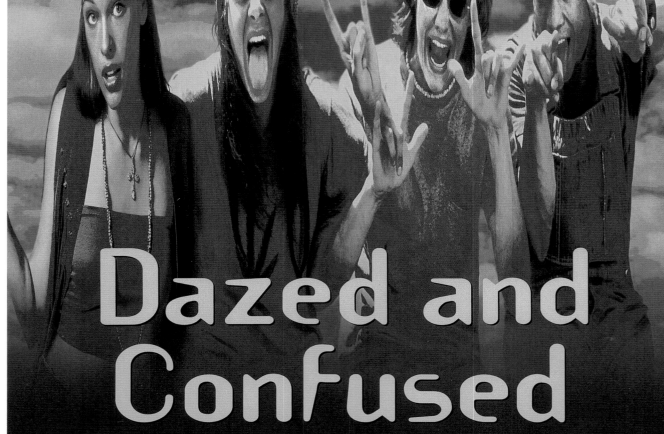

It was the last day of school in 1976
A time they'd never forget
(If only they could remember)

Dazed and Confused

See It With A Bud

GRAMERCY PICTURES Presents An ALPHAVILLE Production In Association With DETOUR FILMPRODUCTION "DAZED AND CONFUSED"

PRODUCTION DESIGN JOHN FRICK   DIRECTOR OF PHOTOGRAPHY LEE DANIEL   CO-PRODUCER ANNE WALKER-McBAY   PRODUCED BY JAMES JACKS   SEAN DANIEL   RICHARD LINKLATER

   WRITTEN AND DIRECTED BY RICHARD LINKLATER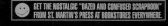

A GRAMERCY PICTURES RELEASE ©1993 Universal City Studios, Inc.

Guy Maddin

Only in Canada's heavily subsidized film industry could a determined eccentric like Guy Maddin find not only acceptance but celebrity. Obsessed with the early years of sound filmmaking, Maddin makes dream-like pastiches of part-talkies set in fairy-tale countries (some of which are named "Canada"). *Tales from the Gimli Hospital* (1988), his first feature, is a tale of the Canadian backwoods that consists largely of characters telling other tales, all rendered in deliberately quaint black-and-white with appropriately scratchy sound. With his 2002 *Dracula*, Maddin expanded his palette to include ballet, filming a performance of a Winnipeg dance troupe in a style that hovers somewhere between German expressionism and Russian montage.

GUY MADDIN
*TALES FROM THE
GIMLI HOSPITAL*
1988
41 x 27 inches
United States

"It's characters may be undead, but the film itself is crazily, passionately alive!"

–A.O. Scott, THE NEW YORK TIMES

a Guy Maddin film

Dracula

Pages from a Virgin's Diary

A Vonnie Von Helmolt Production

A VONNIE VON HELMOLT MARK GODDEN AND GUY MADDIN PRODUCTION EXECUTIVE PRODUCED BY ROBERT SHERRIN FOR THE CANADIAN BROADCASTING CORPORATION IN ASSOCIATION WITH CANADA'S ROYAL WINNIPEG BALLET BASED ON MARK GODDEN'S ORIGINAL BALLET "DRACULA" STARRING ZHANG WEI-QIANG TARA BIRTWHISTLE DAVID MORONI CINDYMARIE SMALL JOHNNY WRIGHT EDITOR AND ASSOCIATE DIRECTOR DECO DAWSON PRODUCTION DESIGN DEANNE ROHDE COSTUME DESIGN PAUL DAIGLE DIRECTOR OF PHOTOGRAPHY PAUL SUDERMAN STILLS BRUCE MONK CO-PRODUCER LESLEY OSWALD ASSOCIATE PRODUCER DANISHKA ESTERHAZY MUSIC COMPOSED BY GUSTAV MAHLER COURTESY NAXOS OF AMERICA POST PRODUCTION BY MIDCANADA PRODUCTION SERVICES PRODUCED WITH THE PARTICIPATION OF THE CANADIAN TELEVISION FUND, TELEFILM CANADA, THE GOVERNMENT OF CANADA AND MANITOBA FILM AND VIDEO PRODUCTION TAX CREDIT PROGRAMS, MANITOBA FILM AND SOUND, CANWEST WESTERN INDEPENDENT PRODUCERS FUND AND WITH THE COLLABORATION OF THE CANADIAN BROADCASTING CORPORATION CHOREOGRAPHER MARK GODDEN PRODUCER VONNIE VON HELMOLT DIRECTOR GUY MADDIN A ZEITGEIST FILMS RELEASE

Zeitgeist
www.zeitgeistfilms.com

Errol Morris

Boston-based documentary-maker Errol Morris has turned his taste for eccentric individuals and bizarre American rites of passage (from pet cemeteries to public executions) into a body of work that both fascinates and disturbs, particularly in its application of fictional storytelling techniques to documentary material. Far from the 1960s' documentary aesthetic of cinema verité, Morris is no detached observer but an active participant in his films, both when he's firing questions from behind the camera (as in *The Fog of War* [2003]) or re-creating episodes for his camera (as in *Mr. Death* [2000]).

ERROL MORRIS
MR. DEATH
2000
41 x 27 inches
United States

ERROL MORRIS
MR. DEATH
2000
41 x 27 inches
United States

AN ERROL MORRIS FILM
BASED ON THE BOOK BY STEPHEN HAWKING

Where did the universe come from?

Will time ever come to an end?

Which came first, the chicken or the egg?

A BRIEF HISTORY OF TIME

TRITON PICTURES RELEASE AN ANGLIA TELEVISION/GORDON FREEDMAN PRODUCTION
IN ASSOCIATION WITH NBC, TOKYO BROADCASTING SYSTEM AND CHANNEL FOUR
AN ERROL MORRIS FILM   A BRIEF HISTORY OF TIME BASED ON THE BOOK BY STEPHEN HAWKING
ORIGINAL MUSIC COMPOSED BY PHILIP GLASS   MUSIC PRODUCED BY KURT MUNKACSI   EDITED BY BRAD FULLER
PRODUCTION DESIGNER TED BAFALOUKOS   DIRECTOR OF PHOTOGRAPHY JOHN BAILEY, A.S.C.   ADDITIONAL PHOTOGRAPHY STEFAN CZAPSKY
EXECUTIVE PRODUCER GORDON FREEDMAN   PRODUCED BY DAVID HICKMAN   DIRECTED BY ERROL MORRIS
©1992 TRITON PICTURES/ANGLIA TELEVISION GORDON FREEDMAN PRODUCTIONS. ALL RIGHTS RESERVED.

FILMED WITH
PANAVISION
CAMERAS & LENSES

BANTAM
READ THE BANTAM BOOK

DOLBY STEREO
IN SELECTED THEATRES

TRITON
PICTURES

Julian Schnabel

One of the most successful painters of the go-go eighties, Julian Schnabel switched gears with his 1996 *Basquiat*, a stylish portrait of a driven young artist who was one of Schnabel's art-world contemporaries. *Before Night Falls* (2000), his second feature, expanded his range to include the verbal artistry of Cuban poet Reinaldo Arenas (Javier Bardem), a victim of Castro's censorship who was finally allowed to immigrate to the United States. As a filmmaker, Schnabel has not yet developed a distinctive signature, but his sheer fearlessness seems likely to propel him toward still more interesting projects.

JULIAN SCHNABEL
BASQUIAT
1996
41 x 27 inches
United States

WINNER/JURY GRAND PRIZE VENICE INTERNATIONAL FILM FESTIVAL
WINNER/Best Actor (Coppa Volpi) JAVIER BARDEM VENICE INTERNATIONAL FILM FESTIVAL

BEFORE

A FILM BY JULIAN SCHNABEL

NIGHT

FALLS

JAVIER BARDEM · OLIVIER MARTINEZ · ANDREA DI STEFANO · JOHNNY DEPP · MICHAEL WINCOTT

JON KILIK PRESENTS A GRANDVIEW PICTURES A FILM BY JULIAN SCHNABEL "BEFORE NIGHT FALLS"
JAVIER BARDEM · OLIVIER MARTINEZ · ANDREA DI STEFANO · JOHNNY DEPP · MICHAEL WINCOTT
CARTER BURWELL ADDITIONAL MUSIC BY LOU REED AND LAURIE ANDERSON MICHAEL BERENBAUM PRODUCTION DESIGNER SALVADOR PARRA
XAVIER PÉREZ GROBET · GUILLERMO ARENAS EXECUTIVE PRODUCERS JULIAN SCHNABEL OLATZ LOPEZ GARMENDIA
CUNNINGHAM O'KEEFE · LÁZARO GÓMEZ CARRILES JULIAN SCHNABEL BASED ON THE MEMOIR BY REINALDO ARENAS
PRODUCED BY JON KILIK JULIAN SCHNABEL

www.before-night-falls.com

Todd Solondz

The apparent cruelty of Todd Solondz's debut feature, 1995's *Welcome to the Dollhouse*, put off many spectators who couldn't see the intense identification between the director and his central character, a miserably unhappy twelve-year-old (Heather Matarazzo) rejected as a hopeless nerd both at home and school. *Happiness* (1998) offered an expanded canvas, a bleakly comic panorama of contemporary American misery that embraced both a lonely substitute teacher (Jane Adams) and a psychiatrist (Dylan Baker) who may also be a psychotic. Solondz refuses to tell the audience how to react to his extreme situations, leaving us to sort out our conflicting feelings of compassion and contempt for ourselves.

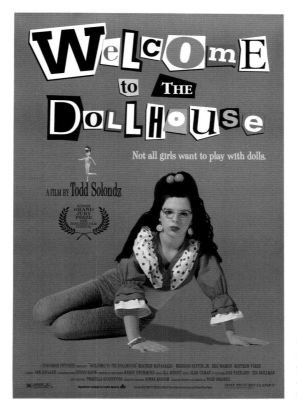

TODD SOLONDZ
WELCOME TO THE DOLLHOUSE
1996
41 x 27 inches
United States

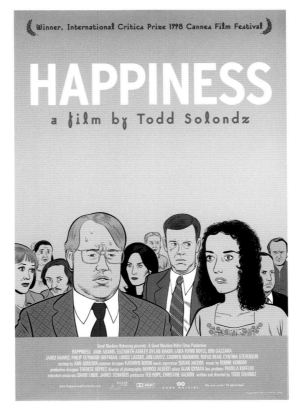

TODD SOLONDZ
HAPPINESS
1998
41 x 27 inches
United States

Quentin Tarantino

The release of *Reservoir Dogs* in 1992 took the American independent cinema in a radical new direction, away from the suffering farmers and anxious teens who had dominated the Sundance Film Festival and toward a new kind of tough-guy cool, forever defined by the Ray-Ban sunglasses and skinny black suits sported by Quentin Tarantino's cast. With 1994's *Pulp Fiction*, Tarantino confirmed his talent with a multithreaded narrative—derived from half-forgotten paperbacks and 1970s action films—that bridged pop culture and high art. His many imitators, dubbed "Taranteenies" by the critics, have obscured his accomplishments, but as a creator of new forms, both visual and narrative, he has few peers in contemporary film.

QUENTIN TARANTINO
PULP FICTION
1994
41 x 27 inches
United States

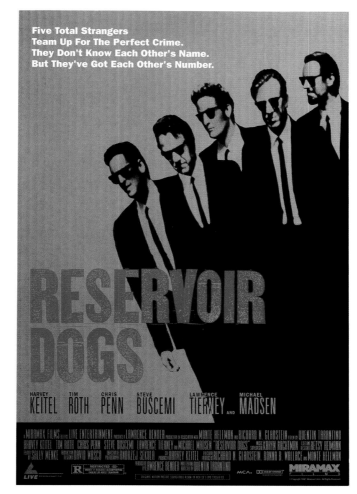

QUENTIN TARANTINO
RESERVOIR DOGS
1992
41 x 27 inches
United States

QUENTIN TARANTINO
RESERVOIR DOGS
1992
39 x 27 inches
Spain

Andrei Tarkovsky

The great Russian visionary filmmaker Andrei Tarkovsky–*Andrei Rublev* (1969), *Solaris* (1972), *Stalker* (1979)–left the U.S.S.R. in 1984, after being told he would no longer be allowed to make his densely metaphorical, metaphysically themed films in the Soviet Union. An outsider among outsiders, the exile Tarkovsky managed to complete only *The Sacrifice* (1986)–a French-Swedish coproduction–before dying of lung cancer in 1986. His long, slow, deliberately repetitive films are not for all tastes, but no sympathetic viewer can resist his hypnotic rhythms and poetic imagery, which mixes Christian symbolism and breathtaking natural landscapes.

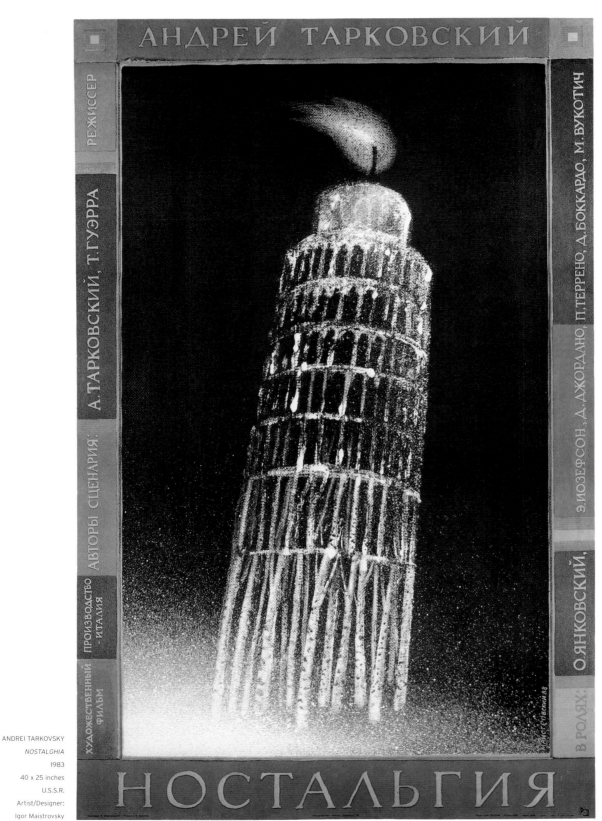

ANDREI TARKOVSKY
NOSTALGHIA
1983
40 x 25 inches
U.S.S.R.
Artist/Designer:
Igor Maistrovsky

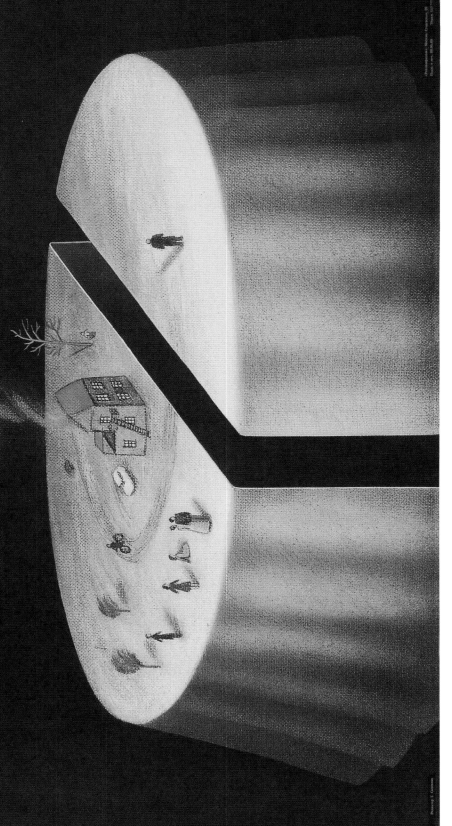

ANDREI TARKOVSKY *STALKER* 1981 63 x 47 inches France Artist/Designer: Bougrine

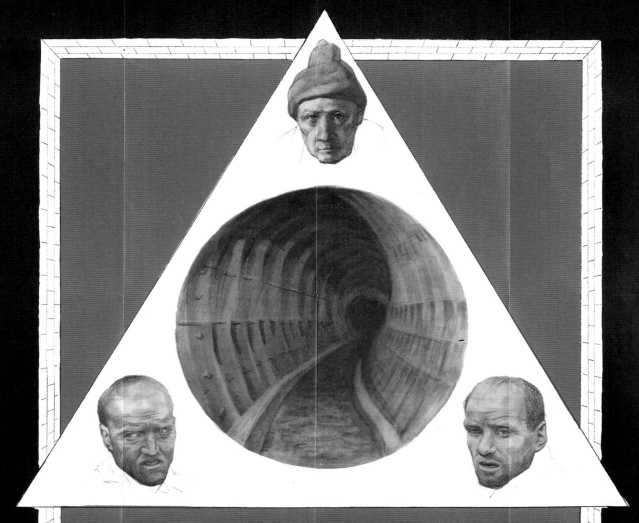

Gus Van Sant

Gus Van Sant first appeared on the indie scene as a pioneer of the New Queer Cinema with his ultra-low budget *Mala Noche* of 1985. Since then, Van Sant has commuted between indie outrageousness (*My Own Private Idaho* [1991], *Gerry* [2002])–and mainstream schlock (*Good Will Hunting* [1997], *Finding Forrester* [2000]) without ever committing himself to a personal esthetic. A gifted chameleon, Van Sant shifts his style to suit his subject.

GUS VAN SANT
MY OWN PRIVATE IDAHO
1991
41 x 27 inches
United States

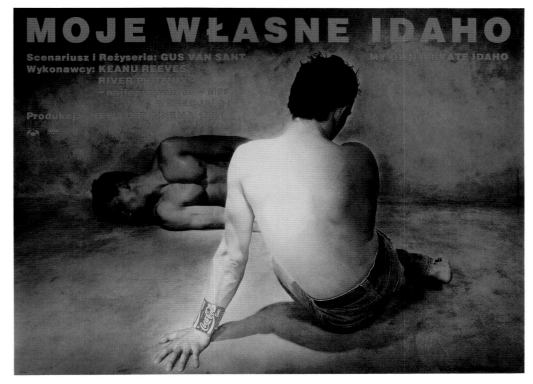

GUS VAN SANT
MY OWN PRIVATE IDAHO
(Moje wlasne Idaho)
1992
26 x 36 inches
Poland
Artist/Designer:
Edmund Lewandowski
and Maciej Mankowski

Lars von Trier

The most controversial European filmmaker of his generation, Lars von Trier has inspired legions of passionate admirers as well as dedicated detractors, who point to the abused heroines of *Breaking the Waves* (1996), *Dancer in the Dark* (2000), and *Dogville* (2003) as examples of violent misogyny. But surely von Trier identifies too ferociously with his put-upon protagonists to be guilty of anything more than ordinary narcissism. One of the first filmmakers to seize the aesthetic possibilities of digital video, von Trier continues to experiment with lighting and framing, and was one of the major architects of the Dogme 95 movement, dedicated to reclaiming the movies from Hollywood's uber-technology and returning them to the simplicity and directness of silent film.

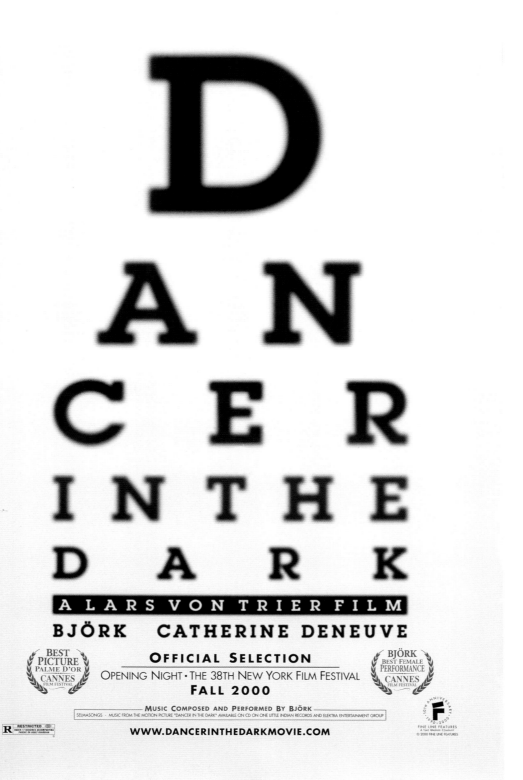

LARS VON TRIER
DANCER IN THE DARK
2000
41 x 27 inches
United States

LARS VON TRIER *THE KINGDOM* 1995 41 x 27 inches United States

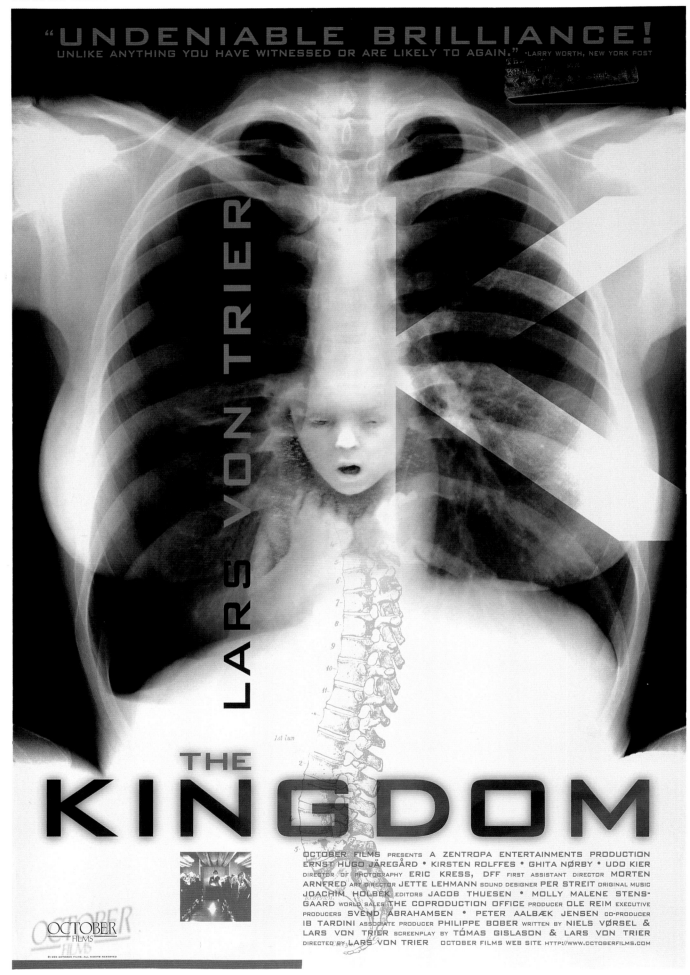

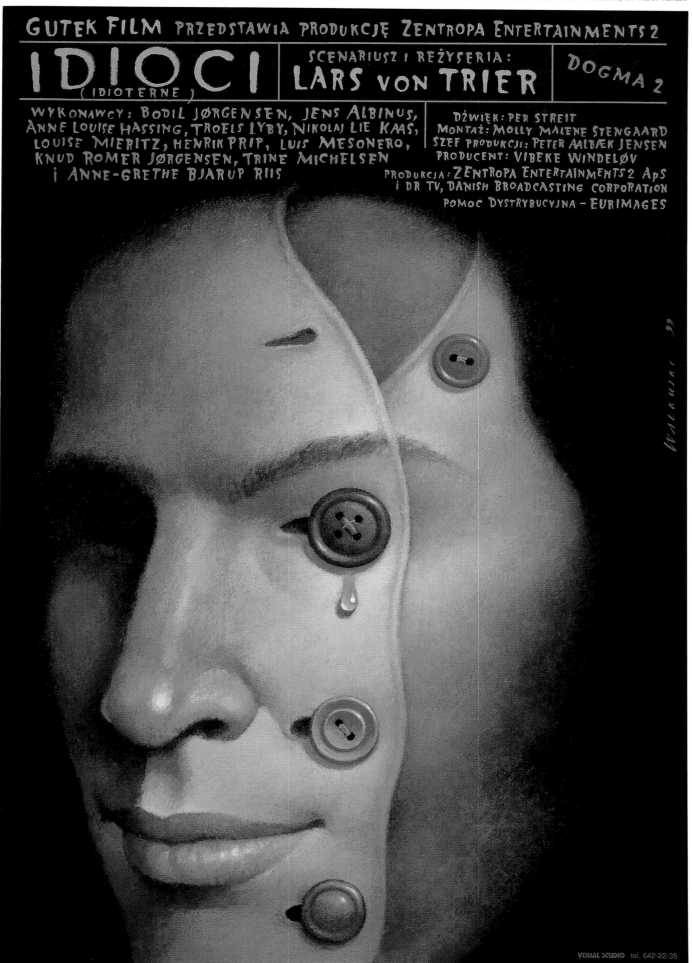

Bruce Weber

Known primarily as a fashion and fine art photographer, Weber has issued a handful of film essays—the most famous of which is *Let's Get Lost* (1988), a meditation on the beautiful-but-doomed jazz trumpeter Chet Baker—that combine outdoorsy Americana and forthright homoeroticism into a style that suggests a gay, hip Norman Rockwell.

BRUCE WEBER
LET'S GET LOST
1988
21 x 17 inches
United States
Photo: William Claxton

BRUCE WEBER
LET'S GET LOST
1988
21 x 17 inches
United States
Photo: William Claxton

BRUCE WEBER
LET'S GET LOST
1988
46 x 37 inches
United States
Photo: William Claxton

BRUCE WEBER
LET'S GET LOST
1988
46 x 37 inches
United States
Photo: William Claxton

Wong Kar Wai

Jim Jarmusch's Chinese cousin, Wong Kar Wai is a tireless creator and purveyor of "hip," defined in his case by sweetly alienated characters, like the two romantically challenged policemen of *Chungking Express* (1994), whose constant pining makes them oblivious to the real opportunities in the world around them. Greatly aided by cinematographer Christopher Doyle, Wong has assembled a visual style as distinctive as Jarmusch's. Wong, however, takes the opposite course, filling his films with clutter and color where Jarmusch strips those elements away. More recent films, such as *Fallen Angels* (1995) and *In the Mood for Love* (2000), play on obsession and repetition as narrative devices, at the risk of a creeping monotony.

WONG KAR WAI
HAPPY TOGETHER
1997
40 x 28 inches
Hong Kong

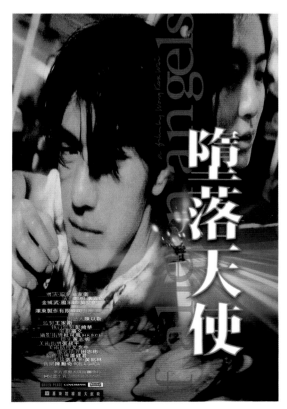

WONG KAR WAI
FALLEN ANGELS
1995
30 x 20 inches
Hong Kong

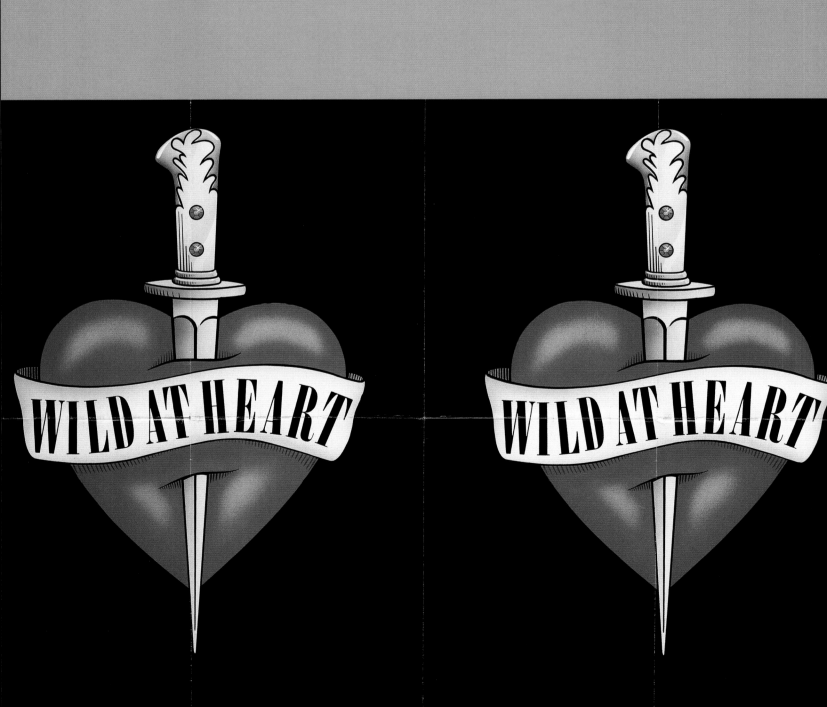

ONE FROM THE HEART:
INDIVIDUAL FILMS

There are filmmakers who come and go passing through independent production on their
way to or from mainstream filmmaking, from the avant-garde and back again, or from
Europe to America or vice versa. If they have not all left behind fully developed, wholly
coherent bodies of work, they have provided many individual moments of pleasure in
the field—and in many cases, some very handsome posters to go with them. Here you'll
find some younger filmmakers, such as Wes Anderson, Danny Boyle, Leos Carax, Sofia
Coppola, David Gordon Green, the team of Scott McGehee and David Siegel, and Lynne
Ramsay and Campbell Scott, whose work is still evolving. You'll also find a number of
European and Asian authors who have had individual successes in the U.S. independent
marketplace, including Theo Angelopoulos from Greece, Hector Babenco from Brazil,
Bruno Dumont from France, Kiyoshi Kurosawa from Japan, Tsai Ming-liang from Taiwan,
and Tom Tykwer from Germany. And then there are the chameleons, filmmakers who
seem to be able to function both within the studio system and, when the mood or
necessity strikes, outside of it: Francis Ford Coppola, Carl Franklin, Dennis Hopper, Neil
Jordan, Ang Lee, David Mamet, Gregory Nava, Sam Raimi, Alfonso Cuarón, and others.

WES ANDERSON
BOTTLE ROCKET
1994
41 x 27 inches
United States

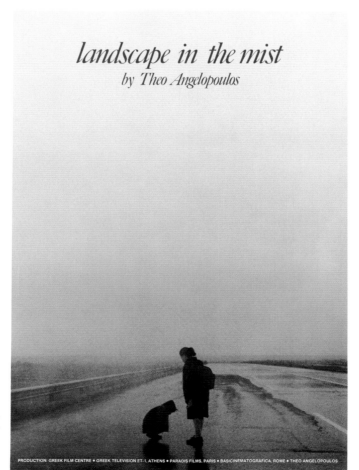

THEO ANGELOPOULOS
LANDSCAPE IN THE MIST
1988
41 x 27 inches
Great Britain

remember those games we used to play?

CHUCK
& BUCK

ARTISAN ENTERTAINMENT AND BLOW UP PICTURES PRESENT A FLAN DE COCO FILM MIKE WHITE CHRIS WEITZ
LUPE ONTIVEROS BETH COLT PAUL WEITZ "CHUCK & BUCK" COSTUME DESIGNER ELAINE MONTALVO COMPOSERS JOEY WARONKER TONY MAXWELL SMOKEY HORMEL EDITOR JEFF BETANCOURT
PRODUCTION DESIGNER RENÉE DAVENPORT DIRECTOR OF PHOTOGRAPHY CHUY CHAVEZ CO-PRODUCERS SCOTT M. CORT BETH COLT CO-EXECUTIVE PRODUCERS THOMAS BROWN CHARLES J. RUSBASAN EXECUTIVE PRODUCERS JASON KLIOT JOANA VICENTE
PRODUCED BY MATTHEW GREENFIELD WRITTEN BY MIKE WHITE DIRECTED BY MIGUEL ARTETA   R   BLOW UP PICTURES   www.chucknbuck.com   ARTISAN ENTERTAINMENT

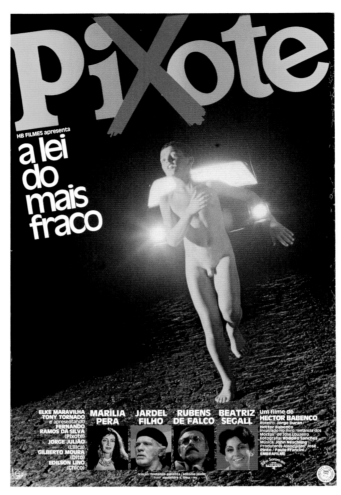

HECTOR BABENCO

PIXOTE

1981

41 x 27 inches

Brazil

MATTHEW BARNEY

THE CREMASTER CYCLE

2002

41 x 27 inches

United States

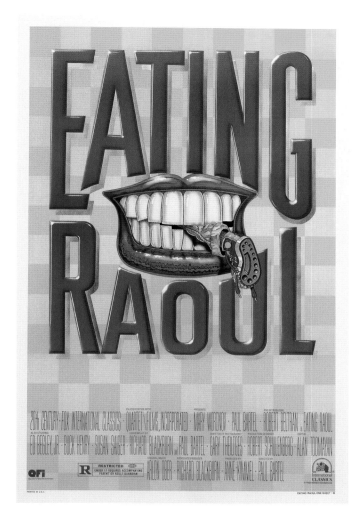

PAUL BARTEL
EATING RAOUL
1982
41 x 27 inches
United States

JEAN-JACQUES BEINEIX
DIVA
1989 rerelease
29 x 20 inches
Japan

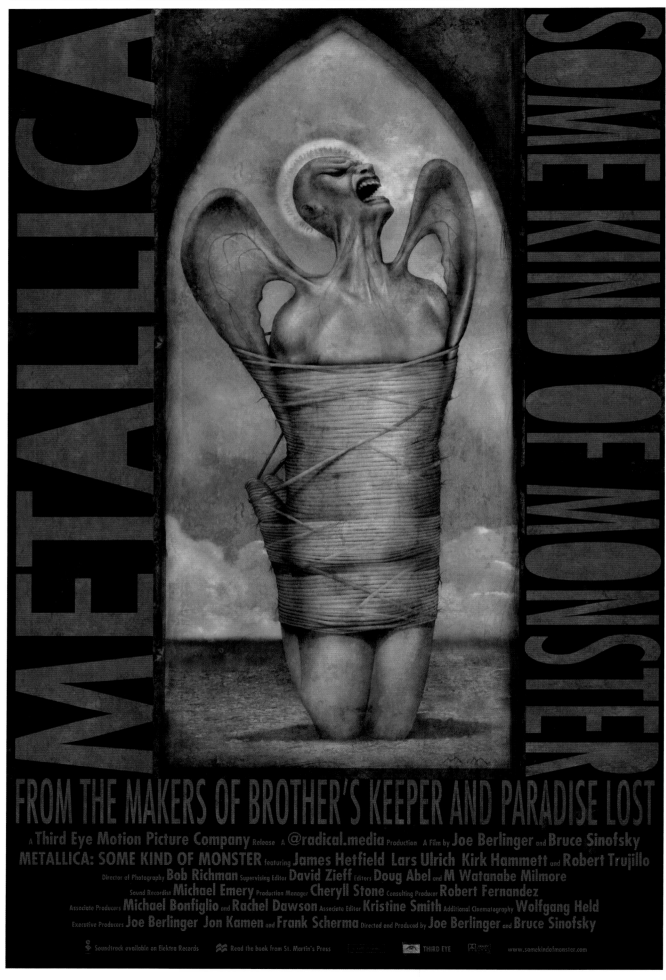

A new provocation from the director of "Romance"

Fat Girl

CATHERINE BREILLAT
FAT GIRL
2001
41 x 27 inches
United States
Artist/Designer: Kim Maley

DANNY BOYLE   *TRAINSPOTTING*   1995   30 x 40 inches   Great Britain   Artist/Designer: Empire Design Company   Photography: Lorenzo Agius

Trainspotting 18

THIS FILM IS EXPECTED TO ARRIVE...

23:02:96

From the team that brought you Shallow Grave

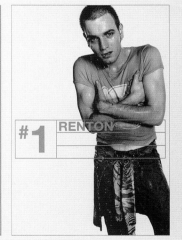

#1 RENTON

#2 BEGBIE

#3 DIANE

#4 SICK BOY

#5 SPUD

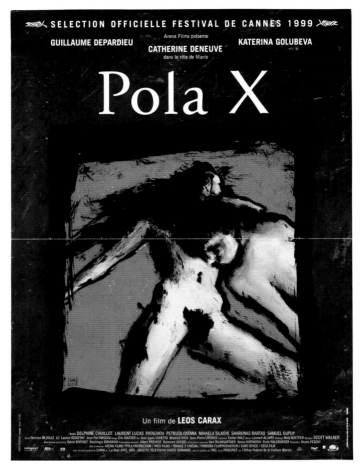

LEOS CARAX
POLA X
1999
20 x 15 inches
France
Artist/Designer: MR

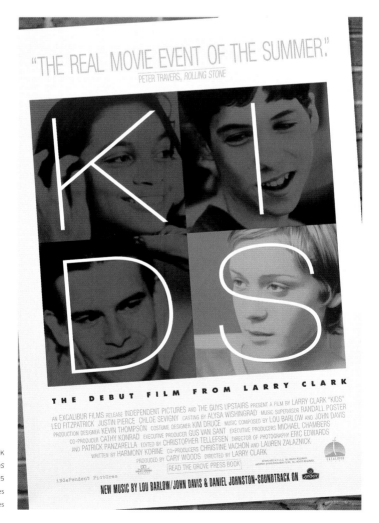

LARRY CLARK
KIDS
1995
41 x 27 inches
United States

SOFIA COPPOLA
LOST IN TRANSLATION
2003
41 x 27 inches
United States

ALFONSO CUARÓN
Y TU MAMÁ TAMBIÉN
2002
41 x 27 inches
United States

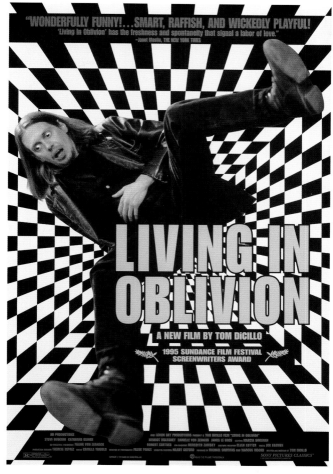

TOM DICILLO
LIVING IN OBLIVION
1995
41 x 27 inches
United States

ERNEST B. DICKERSON *JUICE* 1992 30 x 40 inches Great Britain

Bernd Eichinger zeigt einen **Uli Edel** Film nach dem Buch von **Hubert Selby**

LETZTE AUSFAHRT BROOKLYN

Ich will aufstehen und in der Stadt umhergehen und ihn suchen, den meine Seele liebet.

Das Hohelied Salomos 3, 2–3

Bernd Eichinger zeigt eine **Neue Constantin Film** Produktion in Zusammenarbeit mit **Bavaria Film** und **Allied Filmmakers**
Ein **Uli Edel** Film **Letzte Ausfahrt Brooklyn** · Stephen Lang, Jennifer Jason Leigh, Burt Young, Peter Dobson und Jerry Orbach
Co-Produzent **Herman Weigel** Musik **Mark Knopfler** Schnitt Peter Przygodda Kostüme **Carol Oditz** Bauten **David Chapman**
Kamera **Stefan Czapsky** Nach dem Buch von **Hubert Selby** Drehbuch **Desmond Nakano** Produzent **Bernd Eichinger** Regie **Uli Edel**
Das Buch von Hubert Selby erschienen im ROWOHLT Taschenbuch Verlag. Das Begleitbuch zum Film ist im Buchhandel erhältlich, Verlag: VGS Köln. Original Soundtrack erschienen bei Polygram.

CANNES 1991 • DIRECTORS' FORTNIGHT OFFICIAL SELECTION

In search
of relative
comfort...

A film by Atom Egoyan

THE ADJUSTER

ALLIANCE COMMUNICATIONS CORPORATION PRESENTS
AN EGO FILM ARTS PRODUCTION ⇒ THE ADJUSTER

ELIAS KOTEAS

ARSINÉE KHANJIAN

MAURY CHAYKIN

GABRIELLE ROSE ⇒ DAVID HEMBLEN ⋏ AND JENNIFER DALE

DIRECTOR OF PHOTOGRAPHY	MUSIC BY	CO-PRODUCER	ASSOCIATE PRODUCER
PAUL SAROSSY	MYCHAEL DANNA	CAMELIA FRIEBERG	DAVID WEBB
PRODUCTION DESIGNERS	EDITOR	SOUND DESIGN	WRITTEN & DIRECTED BY
LINDA DEL ROSARIO RICHARD PARIS	SUSAN SHIPTON	STEVEN MUNRO	ATOM EGOYAN

PRODUCED WITH THE FINANCIAL PARTICIPATION OF TELEFILM CANADA AND THE ONTARIO FILM DEVELOPMENT CORPORATION

DOLBY STEREO IN SELECTED THEATRES

ALLIANCE
RELEASING

© 1991 • FAMILY VIEWING PRODUCTIONS LTD. • ALL RIGHTS RESERVED

ABEL FERRARA

THE DIRECTOR OF
KING OF NEW YORK,
BAD LIEUTENANT & THE FUNERAL

"A GENUINE MASTERPIECE"
I-D MAGAZINE

LILI TAYLOR
CHRISTOPHER WALKEN
ANNABELLA SCIORRA

THE ADDICTION 18

EDIE FALCO   PAUL CALDERON   FREDRO STARR   KATHRYN ERBE
MICHAEL IMPERIOLI   JAMEL SIMMONS   NICKY D.   ANTHONY REDMAN A.C.E.   JOHN McINTYRE
"EDITING" JOE DELIA   CREATIVE CONSULTANTS MAYIN LO   FILM EDITOR MARGOT E. LULICK   COSTUME DESIGN MELINDA ESHELMAN
MUSIC JOE DELIA   PHOTOGRAPHY KEN KELSCH   LINE PRODUCER PRESTON HOLMES   ASSOCIATE PRODUCERS ANTHONY BLINKEN   PRODUCTION DESIGN CHARLES LAGOLA
EXECUTIVE PRODUCERS RUSSELL SIMMONS   PRESTON HOLMES   PRODUCED BY DENIS HANN   FERNANDO SULICHIN   LINE PRODUCER MARGOT E. LULICK   MARLA HANSON
WRITTEN BY NICHOLAS ST. JOHN   DIRECTED BY ABEL FERRARA
©1995 OCTOBER FILMS, INC. ALL RIGHTS RESERVED

ABEL FERRARA THE ADDICTION 1995 30 x 40 inches Great Britain

DOLBY STEREO
IN SELECTED THEATRES

MDP

GUILD

117

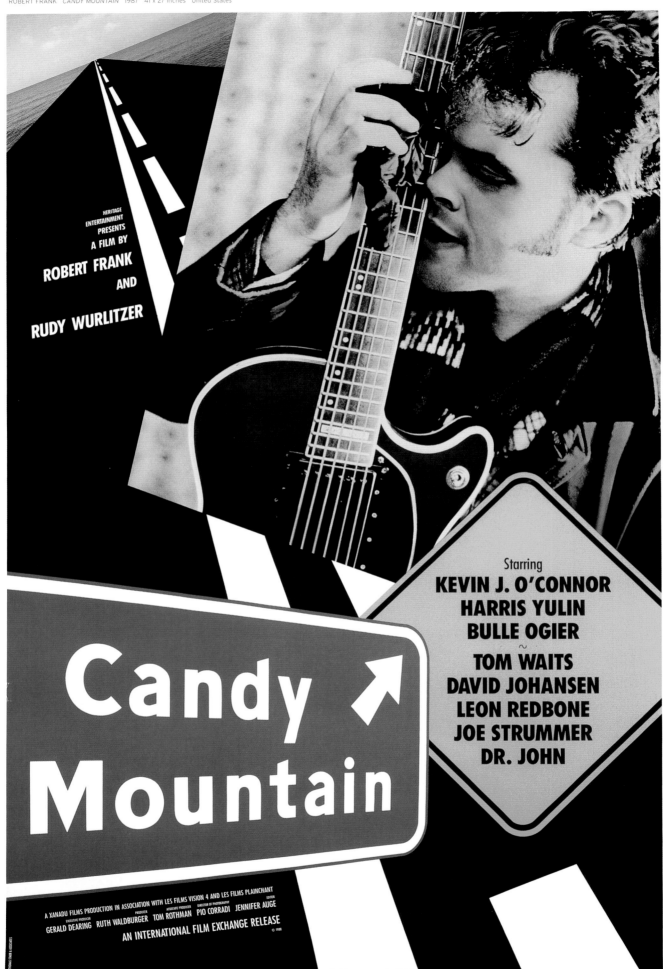

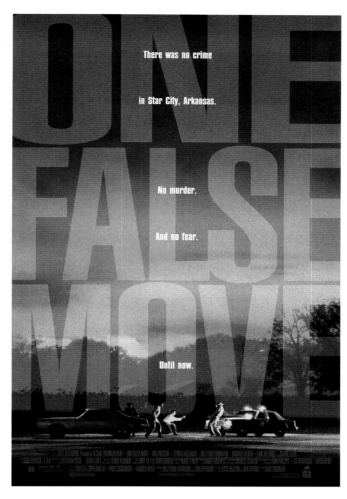

CARL FRANKLIN
ONE FALSE MOVE
1992
41 x 27 inches
United States

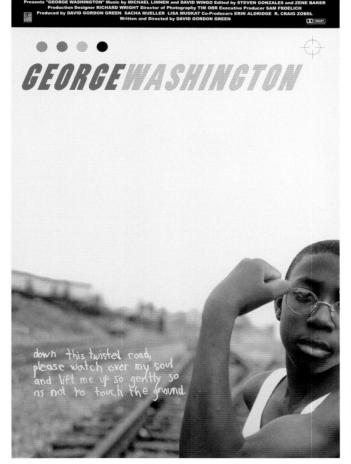

DAVID GORDON GREEN
GEORGE WASHINGTON
2000
41 x 27 inches
United States
Artists/Designers:
Craig Zobel/Dinos and Jake Chapman

WERNER HERZOG
WHERE THE GREEN ANTS DREAM
(Wo die grünen Ameisen träumen)
1984
32 x 23 inches
Germany

MARY HARRON   *I SHOT ANDY WARHOL*   1996   30 x 40 inches   Great Britain

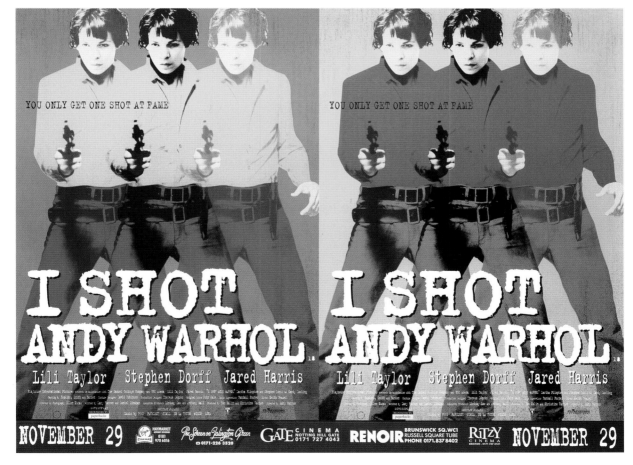

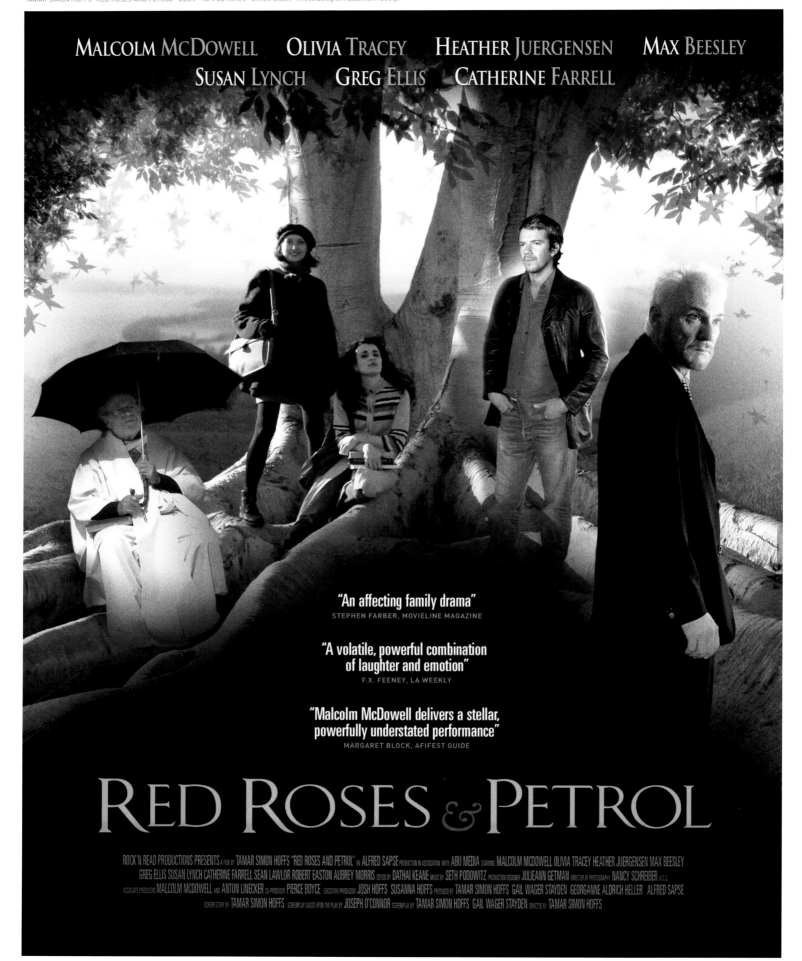

MALCOLM McDOWELL   OLIVIA TRACEY   HEATHER JUERGENSEN   MAX BEESLEY

SUSAN LYNCH   GREG ELLIS   CATHERINE FARRELL

"An affecting family drama"
STEPHEN FARBER, MOVIELINE MAGAZINE

"A volatile, powerful combination
of laughter and emotion"
F.X. FEENEY, LA WEEKLY

"Malcolm McDowell delivers a stellar,
powerfully understated performance"
MARGARET BLOCK, AFIFEST GUIDE

RED ROSES & PETROL

ROCK'N READ PRODUCTIONS PRESENTS A FILM BY TAMAR SIMON HOFFS "RED ROSES AND PETROL" AN ALFRED SAPSE PRODUCTION IN ASSOCIATION WITH ABU MEDIA STARRING MALCOLM McDOWELL OLIVIA TRACEY HEATHER JUERGENSEN MAX BEESLEY GREG ELLIS SUSAN LYNCH CATHERINE FARRELL SEAN LAWLOR ROBERT EASTON AUBREY MORRIS EDITED BY DATHAI KEANE MUSIC BY SETH PODOWITZ PRODUCTION DESIGNER JULIEANN GETMAN DIRECTOR OF PHOTOGRAPHY NANCY SCHREIBER, A.S.C. ASSOCIATE PRODUCERS MALCOLM McDOWELL AND ANTON LINECKER CO-PRODUCER PIERCE BOYCE EXECUTIVE PRODUCERS JOSH HOFFS SUSANNA HOFFS PRODUCED BY TAMAR SIMON HOFFS GAIL WAGER STAYDEN GEORGANNE ALDRICH HELLER ALFRED SAPSE SCREEN STORY BY TAMAR SIMON HOFFS SCREENPLAY BASED UPON THE PLAY BY JOSEPH O'CONNOR SCREENPLAY BY TAMAR SIMON HOFFS GAIL WAGER STAYDEN DIRECTED BY TAMAR SIMON HOFFS

Dennis Hopper's
Out of the Blue x

The "Easy Rider" of the 80's

starring *Linda Manz*
and *Dennis Hopper*

SPIKE JONZE
BEING JOHN MALKOVICH
1999
41 x 27 inches
United States

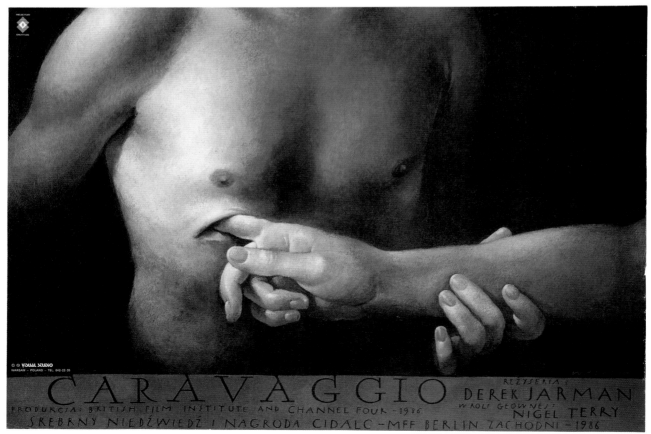

DEREK JARMAN
CARAVAGGIO
1990
27 x 39 inches
Poland
Artist/Designer:
Wieslaw Walkuski

SEX. MURDER. BETRAYAL.
IN NEIL JORDAN'S NEW THRILLER, NOTHING IS WHAT IT SEEMS TO BE.

THE CRYING GAME

...play it at your own risk.

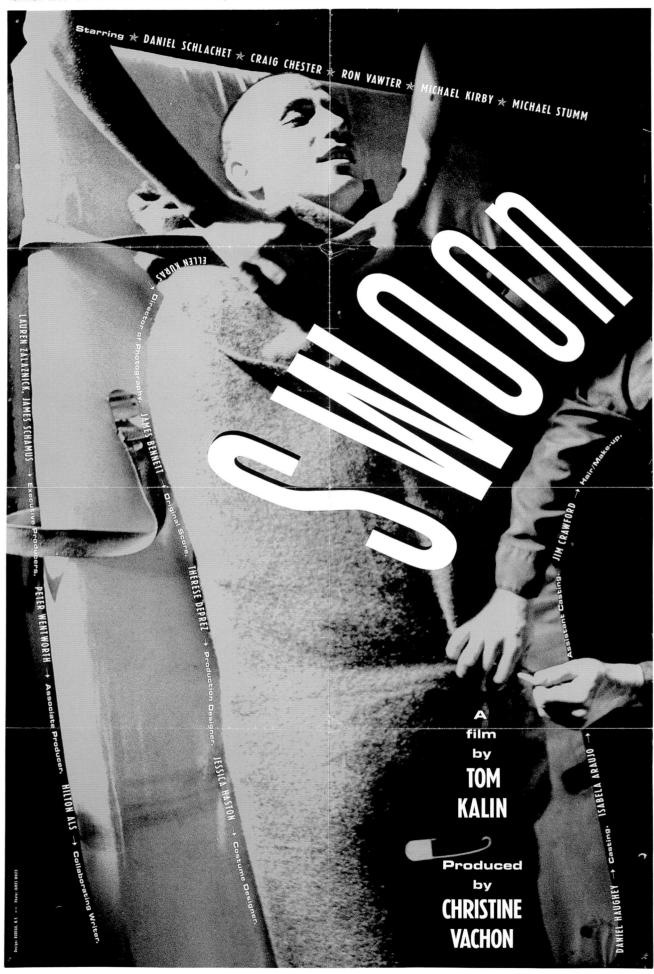

AKIRA KUROSAWA

MADADAYO

1992

29 x 20 inches

Japan

Artist/Designer: Akira Kurosawa

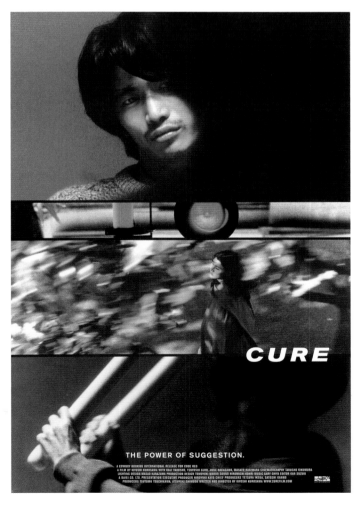

KIYOSHI KUROSAWA

CURE

2001

41 x 27 inches

United States

Artist/Designer: Kim Maley

PRODUCENT: RO FORUM, DISTRIBUCIJA: KINEMA I UNION-FILM
REŽIJA: EMIR KUSTURICA, SCENARIJ: ABDULAH SIDRAN KAMERA: VILKO FILAČ, MUZIKA: ZORAN SIMJANOVIĆ

OTAC NA SLUŽBENOM PUTU

IGRAJU: MORENO DE BARTOLLI, MIKI MANOJLOVIĆ, MIRJANA KARANOVIĆ, MUSTAFA NADAREVIĆ, PAVLE VULJISIĆ,
MIRA FURLAN, PREDRAG LAKOVIĆ, ACE FORČEV, EVA RAS, TOMISLAV GELIĆ, SLOBODAN ALIGRUDIĆ,
EMIR HADŽIHAFIZBEGOVIĆ, DAVOR DUJMOVIĆ, AMER KAPETANOVIĆ,
DESIGN: B. BAĆANOVIĆ, FOTO: B. POPOVIĆ

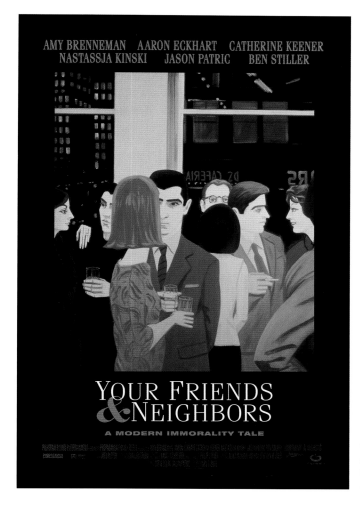

NEIL LABUTE
YOUR FRIENDS AND NEIGHBORS
1998
41 x 27 inches
United States
Artist/Designer: Blair Green

ANG LEE   *EAT DRINK MAN WOMAN*   1994   30 x 40 inches   Great Britain

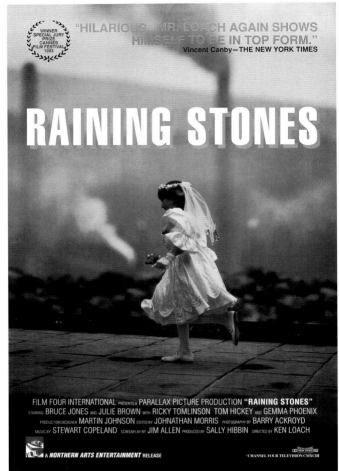

KEN LOACH
RAINING STONES
1993
41 x 27 inches
United States

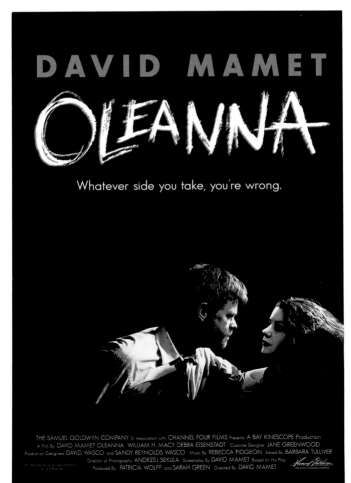

DAVID MAMET
OLEANNA
1994
41 x 27 inches
Great Britain

LUCRECIA MARTEL
LA CIÉNAGA
2001
41 x 27 inches
United States
Artist/Designer: Kim Maley

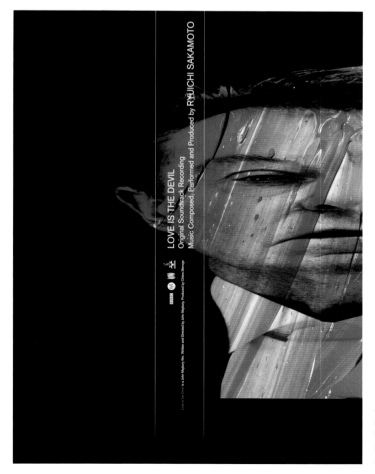

JOHN MAYBURY
LOVE IS THE DEVIL
1998
24 x 18 inches
Great Britain

TSAI MING-LIANG
VIVE L'AMOUR
(*Aiqing wansui*)
1995
29 x 20 inches
Japan
Artist/Designer:
Tadanori Yokoo

SCOTT MCGEHEE,
DAVID SIEGEL
SUTURE
1993
30 x 40 inches
Great Britain

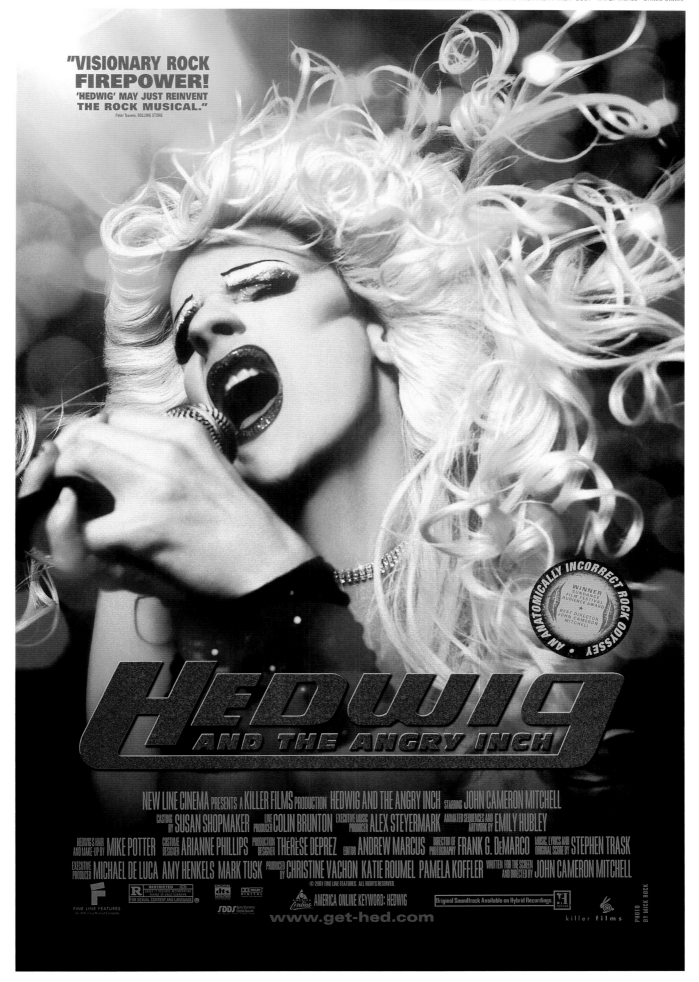

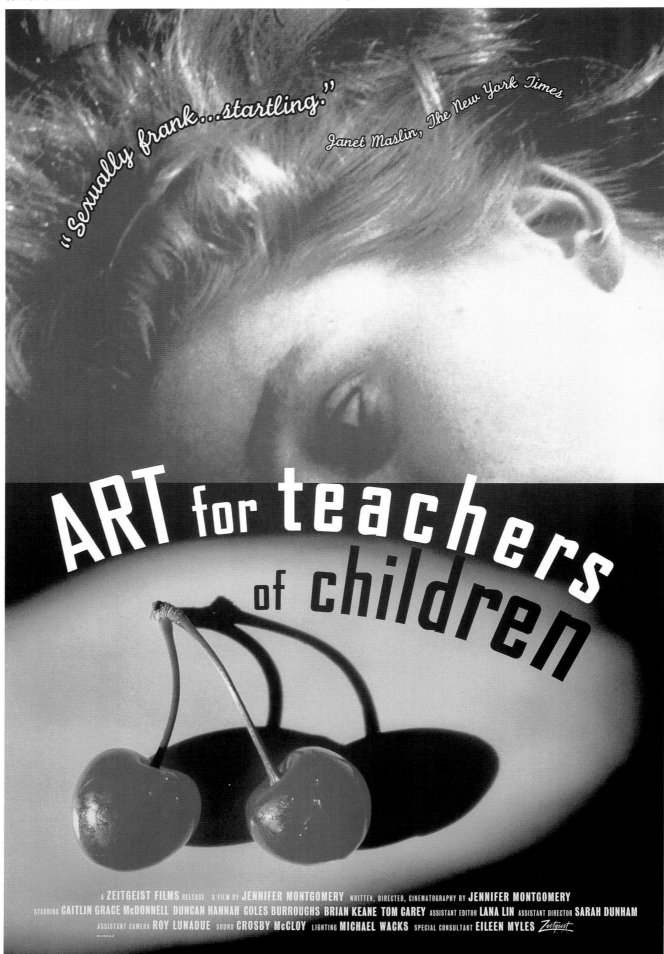

"Sexually frank…startling."

Janet Maslin, The New York Times

ART for teachers of children

A ZEITGEIST FILMS RELEASE A FILM BY JENNIFER MONTGOMERY WRITTEN, DIRECTED, CINEMATOGRAPHY BY JENNIFER MONTGOMERY
STARRING CAITLIN GRACE McDONNELL DUNCAN HANNAH COLES BURROUGHS BRIAN KEANE TOM CAREY ASSISTANT EDITOR LANA LIN ASSISTANT DIRECTOR SARAH DUNHAM
ASSISTANT CAMERA ROY LUNADUE SOUND CROSBY McCLOY LIGHTING MICHAEL WACKS SPECIAL CONSULTANT EILEEN MYLES Zeitgeist

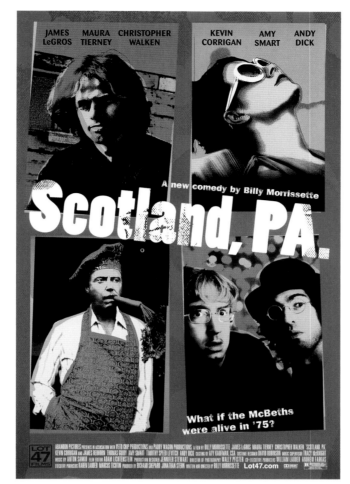

BILLY MORRISSETTE
SCOTLAND, PA.
2001
41 x 27 inches
United States

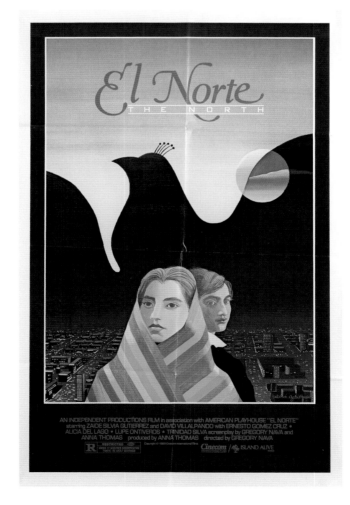

GREGORY NAVA
EL NORTE
1983
41 x 27 inches
United States

GREG NICKSON *DRUM STRUCK* 1991 30 x 22 inches United States

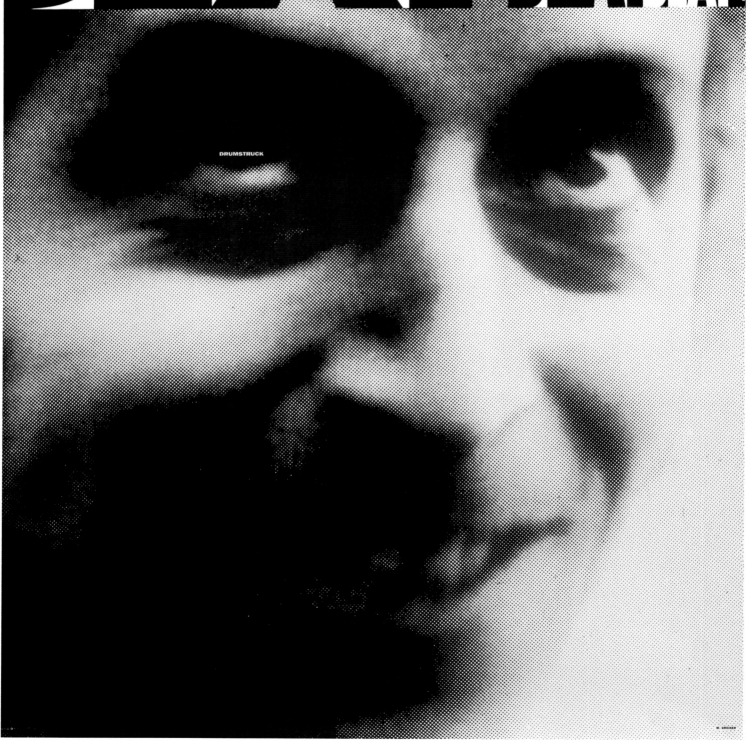

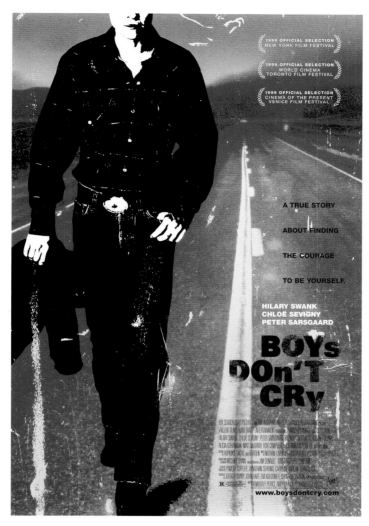

KIMBERLY PIERCE
BOYS DON'T CRY
1999
41 x 27 inches
United States

GASPAR NOÉ
I STAND ALONE
(Seul contre tous)
1998
30 x 40 inches
Great Britain
Artists/Designers:
Dinos and Jake Chapman

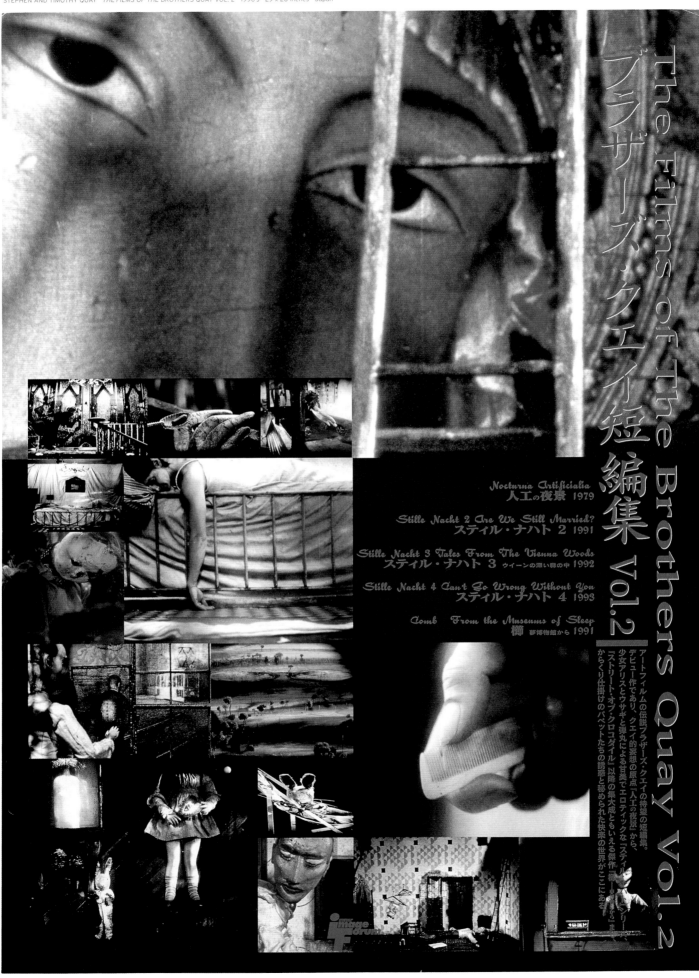

Nocturna Artificialia
人工の夜景 1979

Stille Nacht 2 Are We Still Married?
スティル・ナハト 2 1991

Stille Nacht 3 Tales From The Vienna Woods
スティル・ナハト 3 ウィーンの深い森の中 1992

Stille Nacht 4 Can't Go Wrong Without You
スティル・ナハト 4 1993

Comb   From the Museums of Sleep
櫛 夢博物館から 1991

SAM RAIMI
THE EVIL DEAD
1983
63 x 47 inches
France
Artist/Designer: C. Lalande

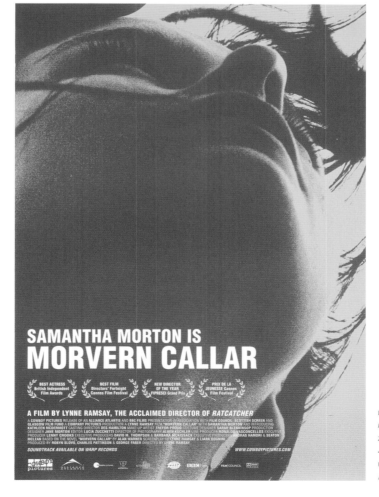

LYNNE RAMSAY
MORVERN CALLAR
2002
41 x 27 inches
United States
Artist/Designer: Kim Maley

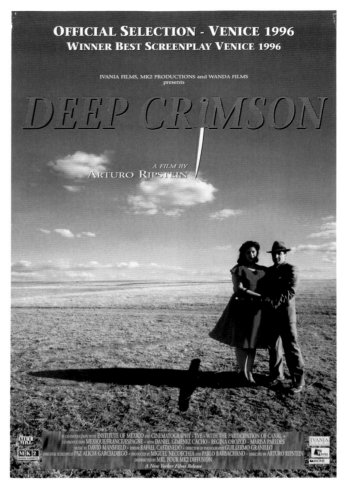

ARTURO RIPSTEIN
DEEP CRIMSON
1996
41 x 27 inches
United States

BRUCE ROBINSON
WITHNAIL AND I
1986
41 x 27 inches
Great Britain
Artist/Designer:
Ralph Steadman

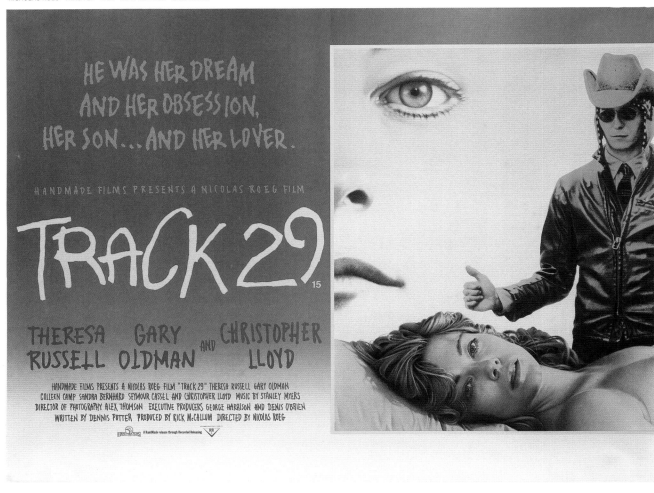

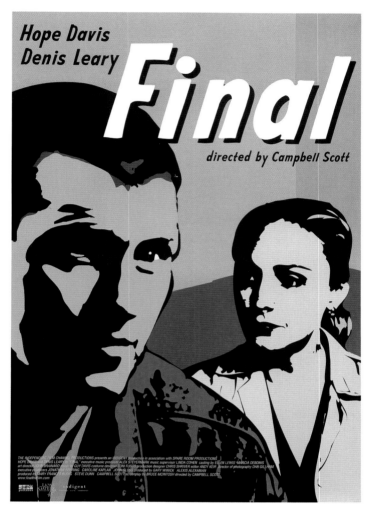

CAMPBELL SCOTT
FINAL
2001
41 x 27 inches
United States
Artist/Designer: Kim Maley

SUSAN SEIDELMAN
SMITHEREENS
1982
22 x 17 inches
United States

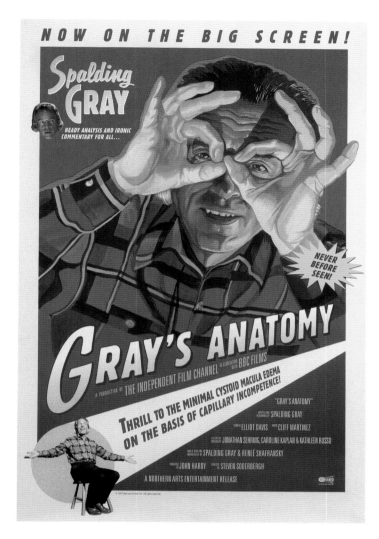

STEVEN SODERBERGH
GRAY'S ANATOMY
1997
41 x 27 inches
United States

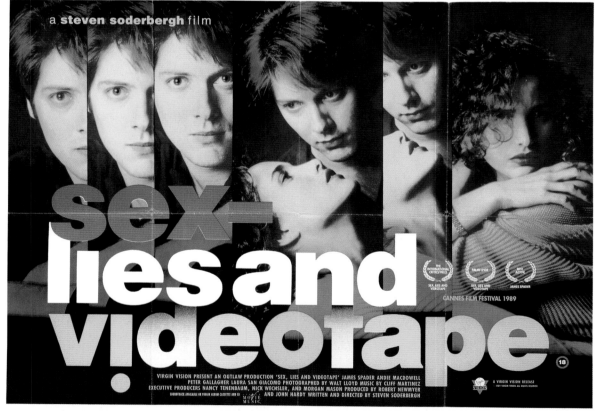

STEVEN SODERBERGH
SEX, LIES,
AND VIDEOTAPE
1989
30 x 40 inches
Great Britain

JAN SVANKMAJER
CONSPIRATORS OF PLEASURE
(*Spiklenci slasti*)
1996
34 x 23 inches
Czech Republic
Artist/Designer:
Eva Svankmerova

JULIE TAYMOR
FRIDA
2002
41 x 27 inches
United States

BILLY BOB THORNTON
SLING BLADE
1996
41 x 27 inches
United States

ROSE TROCHE
GO FISH
1994
41 x 27 inches
United States

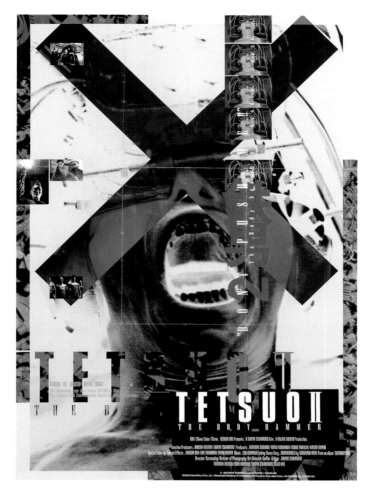

SHINYA TSUKAMOTO
TETSUO II, THE BODY HAMMER
1991
40 x 29 inches
Japan

SLAVA TSUKERMAN
LIQUID SKY
1982
41 x 27 inches
United States

Jeden Tag
Jede Sekunde
triffst Du eine Entscheidung
die Dein Leben verändern kann

Ein Film von *Tom Tykwer*

lola*rennt*

mit FRANKA POTENTE

MORITZ BLEIBTREU

X-Filme Creative Pool präsentiert »Lola rennt« mit Franka Potente und Moritz Bleibtreu sowie Herbert Knaup
Nina Petri Joachim Król Armin Rohde Heino Ferch Suzanne von Borsody Sebastian Schipper u.v.a.
Kamera Frank Griebe Schnitt Mathilde Bonnefoy Ton Frank Behnke Tonmischung Matthias Lempert
Musik Tom Tykwer Johnny Klimek Reinhold Heil Ausstattung Alexander Manasse Kostüme Monika Jacobs
Redaktion Gebhard Henke (WDR) und Andreas Schreitmüller (arte)
Produktionsleitung Ralph Brosche Herstellungsleitung Maria Köpf Produzent Stefan Arndt Buch und Regie Tom Tykwer

Das Buch zum Film ist erhältlich beim ROWOHLT VERLAG

ORIGINAL-SOUNDTRACK erhältlich über

Die Single »WISH« mit Franka Potente & Thomas D. ist erschienen bei

Der Film wurde gefördert von   und vom BUNDESMINISTERIUM DES INNERN

www.lolarennt.de

THE RED SIDE OF LIFE

Ein X-Filme Creative Pool-Film im Verleih von PROKINO/MEDIA PART

AN UNFORGETTABLE COMEDY FROM THE DIRECTOR OF "CRUMB"

Accentuate
the
negative.

A TERRY ZWIGOFF FILM

GHOST WORLD

UNITED ARTISTS FILMS AND GRANADA FILM IN ASSOCIATION WITH JERSEY SHORE PRESENT A MR. MUDD PRODUCTION A TERRY ZWIGOFF FILM "GHOST WORLD" THORA BIRCH
SCARLETT JOHANSSON BRAD RENFRO WITH ILLEANA DOUGLAS AND STEVE BUSCEMI LINE PRODUCER BARBARA A. HALL EXECUTIVE PRODUCERS PIPPA CROSS JANETTE DAY COSTUME DESIGNER MARY ZOPHRES
EDITOR CAROLE KRAVETZ PRODUCTION DESIGNER EDWARD T. McAVOY DIRECTOR OF PHOTOGRAPHY AFFONSO BEATO PRODUCED BY LIANNE HALFON JOHN MALKOVICH RUSSELL SMITH
www.mgm.com BASED ON THE COMIC BOOK BY DANIEL CLOWES WRITTEN BY DANIEL CLOWES & TERRY ZWIGOFF DIRECTED BY TERRY ZWIGOFF DISTRIBUTED BY MGM DISTRIBUTION CO.

THE STATE OF THINGS:
TRUTH, DOCUMENTARY STYLE

Documentary film has been an important part of the indie movement since its inception. From the start, when it was still known as the USA Film Festival, Sundance has placed documentaries on the same level, for prestige and prizes as fiction films, a revolutionary stance that has since become standard. Among the progenitors of indie docs are Nick Broomfield and his guerrilla-documentaries, approaching their subjects by stealth and taking them in ambush; Jennie Livingston, whose *Paris Is Burning* (1990) introduced a gay sensibility to a field dominated by the determinedly straight; and Jayne Loader, Kevin Rafferty, and Pierce Rafferty, whose witty compilation of government Cold War propaganda, *The Atomic Cafe* (1982), established a new, ironic discourse for the documentary, and probably paved the way for both the agit-prop cinema of Michael Moore and the cozy, film-clip nostalgia of Ken Burns.

KARIM AïNOUZ
MADAME SATÃ
2002
41 x 27 inches
United States
Artist/Designer:
Amy Crownover

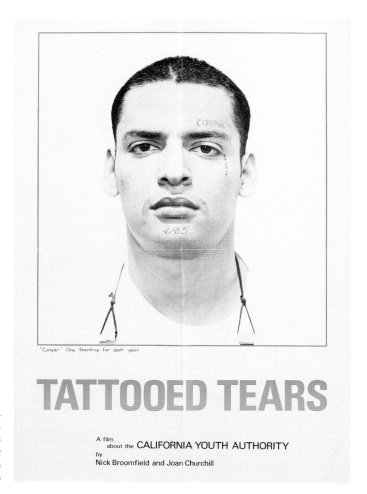

NICK BROOMFIELD,
JOAN CHURCHILL
TATTOOED TEARS
1982
24 x 17 inches
Great Britain

"Extraordinarily vivid! Adheres to the finest
traditions of the storyteller's art. See it!"
–Orlando Weekly

A FILM BY PAUL DEVLIN

Slam NATION

THE SPORT OF SPOKEN WORD

SLAMMIN' ENTERTAINMENT PRESENTS A FILM BY PAUL DEVLIN
SAUL WILLIAMS JESSICA CARE MOORE MUMS THE SCHEMER BEAU SIA TAYLOR MALI AND FEATURING MARC SMITH 'FATHER OF THE SLAM'
CO-PRODUCERS TOM POOLE & MICHAEL SHAW EDITING MAXIME GIORDANI DIRECTOR OF PHOTOGRAPHY JOHN ANDERSON AUDIO JOHN KAYNE DIRECTED AND PRODUCED BY PAUL DEVLIN

OPENS FRIDAY JULY 17 @ FILM FORUM
HOUSTON ST. (W OF 6TH AV)   727-8110   WWW.FILMFORUM.COM   DAILY AT 2, 4, 6, 8, 10 **LIVE POETRY**

KIRBY DICK   *SICK: THE LIFE & DEATH OF BOB FLANAGAN, SUPERMASOCHIST*   1997   41 x 27 inches   Canada   Photo: Sheree Rose   Artist/Designer: Rita Valencia

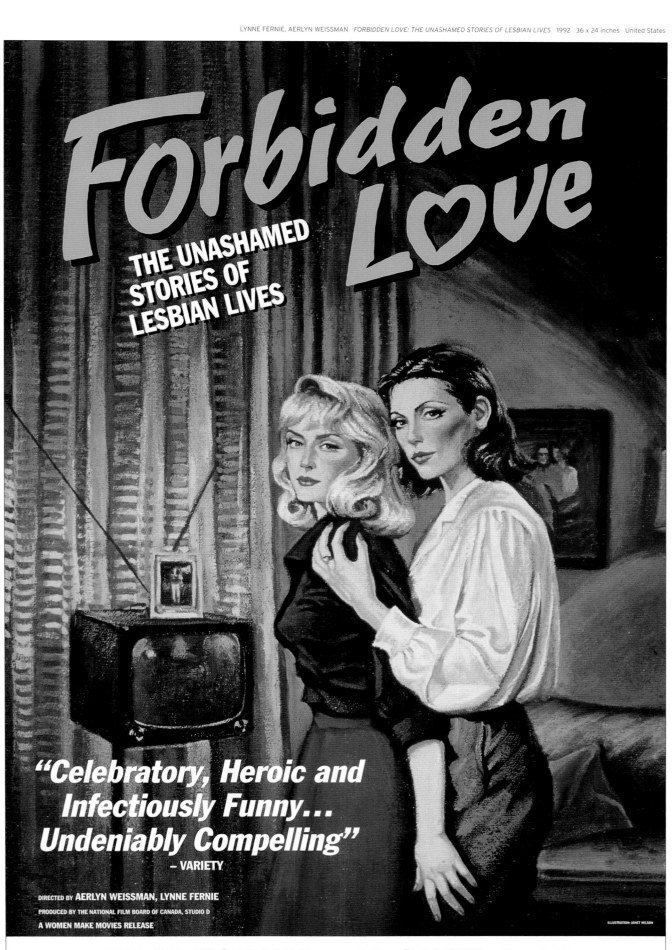

STRAND RELEASING PRESENTS

BEEFCAKE

A FILM BY THOM FITZGERALD

FROM THE ACCLAIMED
DIRECTOR OF
THE HANGING GARDEN

Strand Releasing presents in association with
Alliance Atlantis, Channel Four Television,
La Sept Arte, Mikado Films and Odeon Films
An Emotion Picture BEEFCAKE
Inspired by the book by F. Valentine Hooven III
Starring Daniel MacIvor Carroll Godsman J. Griffin Mazeika
Jonathan Torrens and Josh Peace with Jack LaLanne and Joe Dallesandro
Photo Montage Animator Dominique Parizeau Costume Designer James A. Worthen
Music Composed by John Roby Michael Diabo John Wesley Chisholm
Edited by Susan Shanks and Michael Weir
Production Designer D'Arcy Poultney
Director of Photography Thomas M. Harting
Line Producer Tara Cowell-Plain
Associate Producers Barbara Badessi Marc Betsworth Dreux Ellis James Nicholson
Produced by Thom Fitzgerald and Shandi Mitchell
Written and Directed by Thom Fitzgerald

RECORDED IN
ULTRA STEREO

www.strandrel.com
©1999 STRAND RELEASING

STRAND
RELEASING

JENNIE LIVINGSTON *PARIS IS BURNING* 1991 27 x 22 inches United States

PARIS IS BURNING

**GRAND JURY PRIZE
1991 SUNDANCE FILM FESTIVAL**

**BEST DOCUMENTARY OF 1990
LOS ANGELES
FILM CRITICS' ASSOCIATION**

**Directed and Produced
by Jennie Livingston**

**Edited by
Jonathan Oppenheim**

**Cinematography
by Paul Gibson**

**Co-produced
by Barry Swimar**

Partially funded by Art Matters, Inc., the British Broadcasting Corporation, the Edelman Family Fund, the New York Foundation for the Arts, the New York State Council on the Arts, the National Endowment for the Arts, and the Paul Robeson Fund.

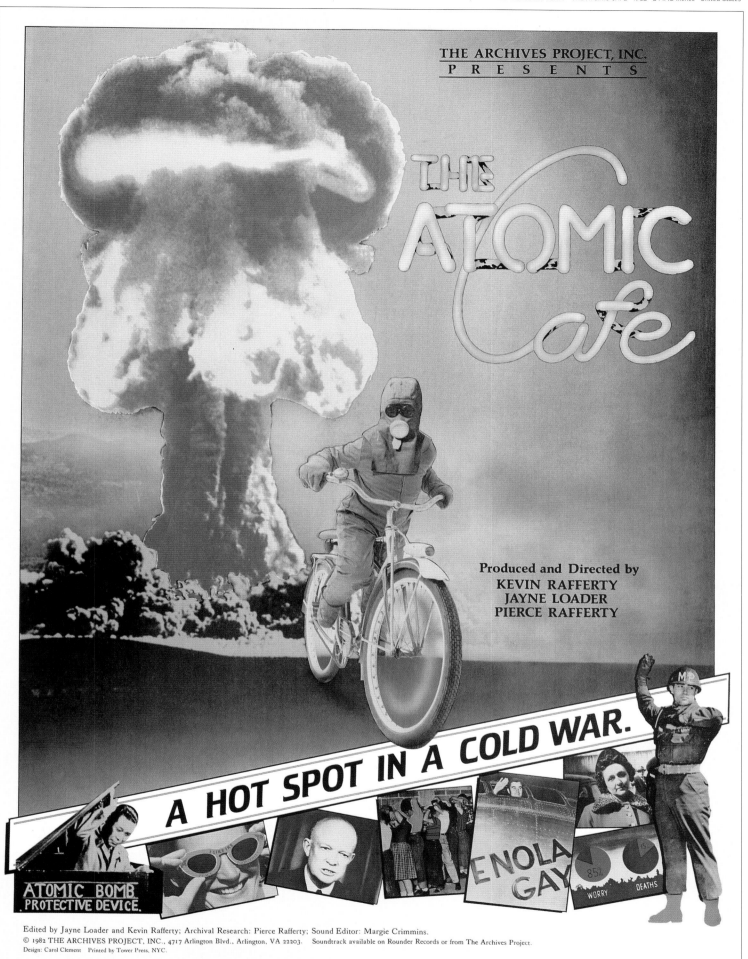

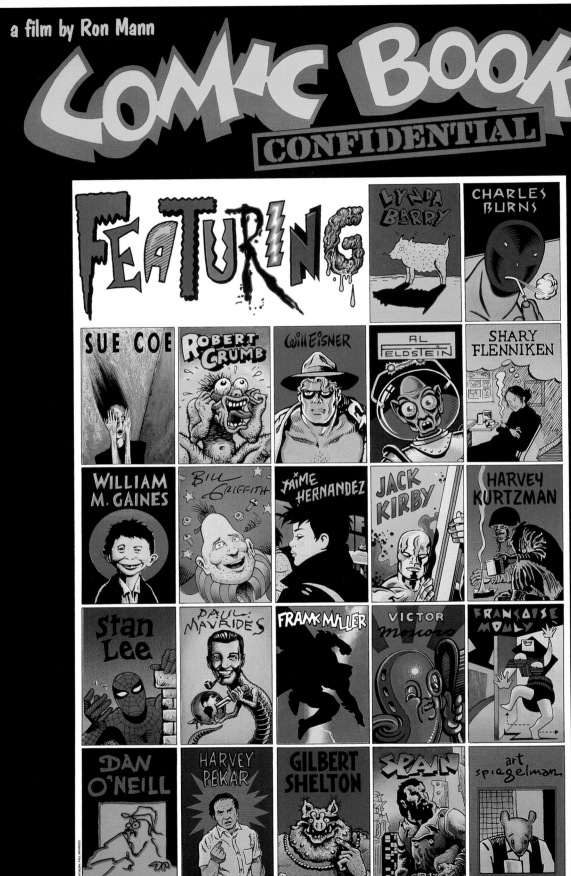

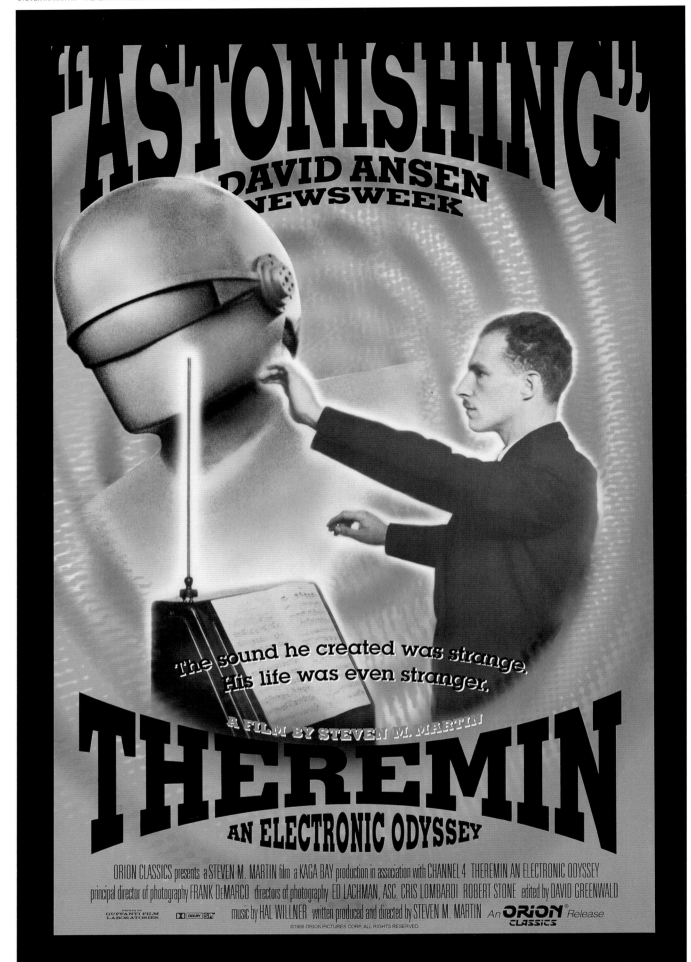

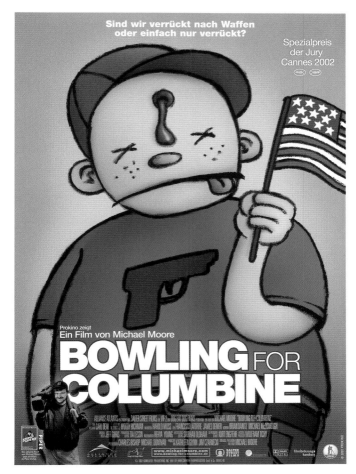

MICHAEL MOORE
BOWLING FOR COLUMBINE
2002
32 x 23 inches
Germany
Artist/Designer: Prokino

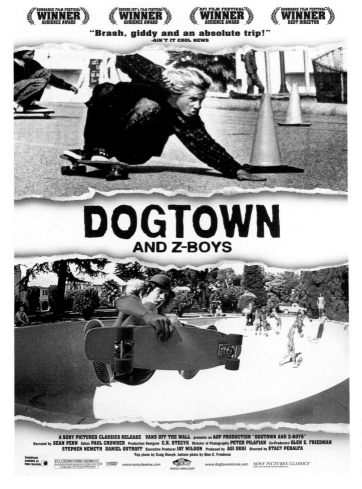

STACY PERALTA
DOGTOWN AND Z-BOYS
2001
41 x 27 inches
United States

GODFREY REGGIO
KOYAANISQATSI
1983
29 x 20 inches
Japan
Artist/Designer:
Haruo Takino

PETER SCHAMONI
NIKI DE SAINT PHALLE
1996
33 x 23 inches
Germany

BARRY SHILS
WIGSTOCK: THE MOVIE
1995
41 x 27 inches
United States

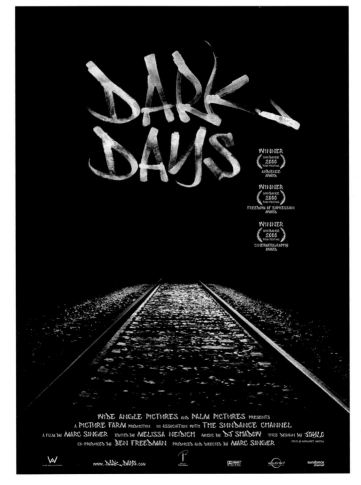

MARC SINGER
DARK DAYS
2000
41 x 27 inches
United States

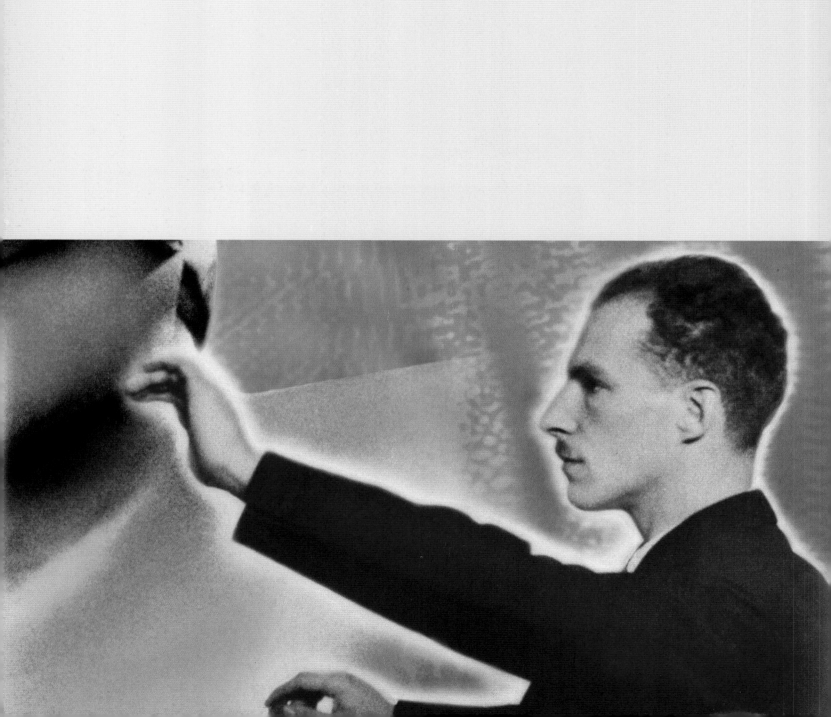

LET'S GET LOST:
MUSIC MOVIES

Music, like the movies, has its outlaws, and if Elvis was the king of Hollywood rockers, the ruling figures in independent music documentaries became edgier acts like the Talking Heads, the Sex Pistols, and Laurie Anderson. Many of these musicians would never have stood a chance of reaching the screen without independent filmmakers to back them up: The punk movement survives, not in high-gloss Hollywood fictions but in gritty documentaries like Lech Kowalski's *D.O.A.* (1980) and Penelope Spheeris's *The Decline of Western Civilization* (in three parts: 1981, 1988, and 1998). And rebels from the past have been preserved as well: the indie rock icon Nico, the doomed jazz trumpeter and vocalist Chet Baker, the uncategorizable piano genius Thelonious Monk. More recently, the Chicago alternative band Wilco found its cinematic voice in Sam Jones's modest and lovely tribute, *I Am Trying to Break Your Heart* (2002).

LAURIE ANDERSON *HOME OF THE BRAVE: A FILM BY LAURIE ANDERSON*
1986   60 x 20 inches   Great Britain

JONATHAN DEMME *STOP MAKING SENSE* 1984   41 x 27 inches   United States

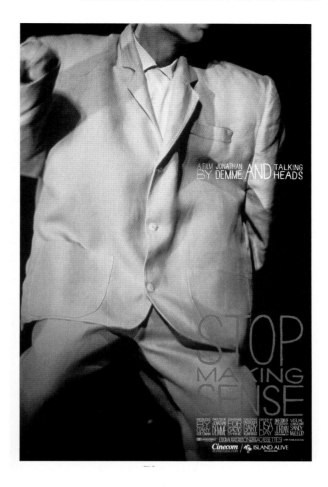

SAM JONES   *I AM TRYING TO BREAK YOUR HEART*   2002   41 x 27 inches   United States

MICHAEL GRAMAGLIA, JIM FIELDS   *END OF THE CENTURY: THE STORY OF THE RAMONES*   2004   40 x 27 inches   United States   Artist/Designer: Peter Vacca, Arnie Sawyer Studios, Inc.

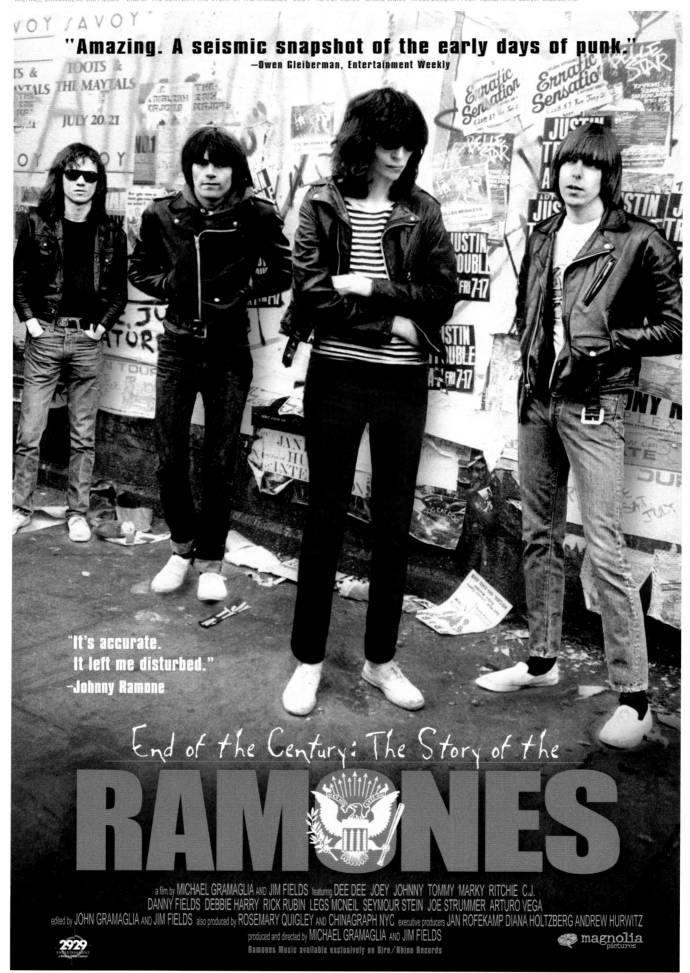

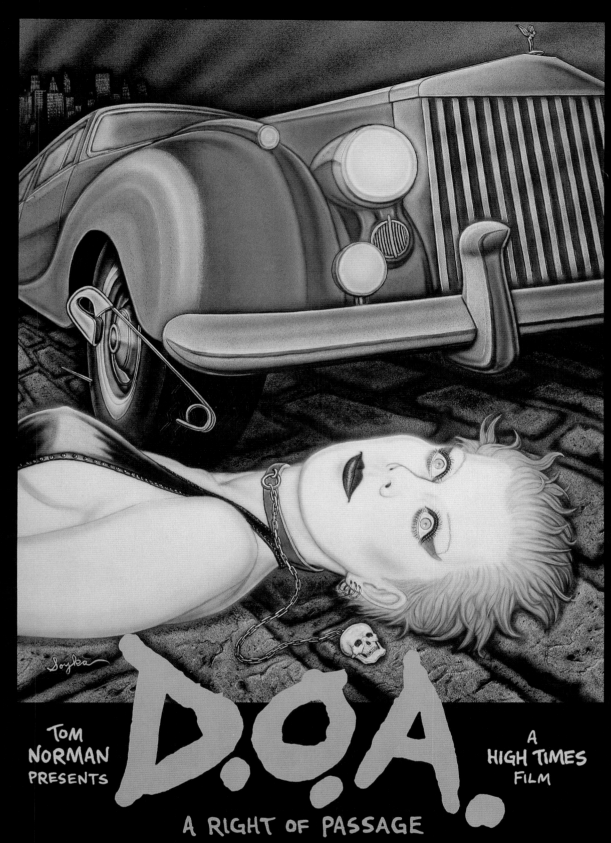

THE DECLINE
of western civilization

filmed December 1979 through May 1980 Los Angeles, CA

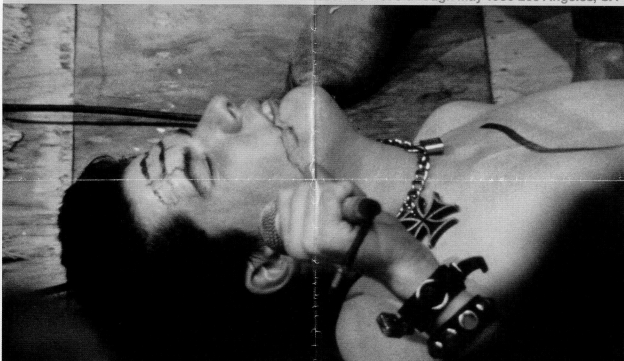

©Spheeris Films, Inc. 1980

Spheeris Films Inc.
presents

**ALICE BAG BAND   BLACK FLAG   CATHOLIC DISCIPLINE
CIRCLE JERKS   FEAR   GERMS
and X**

Produced and Directed by Penelope Spheeris   Executive Producers: Gordon Brown and Jeff Prettyman

SOUNDTRACK LP ON SLASH RECORDS

Poster Design – J. Ruby Prods. Inc.

JULIEN TEMPLE
THE FILTH AND THE FURY
1999
41 x 27 inches
United States

CHARLOTTE ZWERIN
THELONIOUS MONK:
STRAIGHT, NO CHASER
1989
41 x 27 inches
United States
Artist/Designer:
Jim Hedden and Bill Gold